LEAD FROM THE HEART UP, NOT THE NECK UP:

*How to create a Positive,
Winning culture on the field and in the office*

Claudio Reilsono

Copyright 2020
by Claudio Reilsono. All rights reserved

Published by:

John Melvin Publishing, LLC

344 St. Joseph St.

Suite 538

New Orleans, LA 70130

www.johnmelvinpublishing.com

ISBN: 978-1-7351627-2-0 Paperback

978-1-7351627-3-7 Kindle Edition

Library of Congress Control Number: 2020917707

Cover Design by; Lizzie Schinkel

No part of this work may be reproduced or transmitted in any form or by any means, electronic, manual, photocopying, recording, or by any information storage and retrieval system, without prior written permission of the publisher.

Printed in the United States of America

TABLE OF CONTENTS

Dedication 1

Introduction 2

Forward 5

Chapter 1: The Cold Shoulder 6

Chapter 2: The Wrong Door 8

Chapter 3: He Was There… But He Wasn't There .. 11

Chapter 4: Music To The Ears: Part 1 13

Chapter 5: Music To The Ears: Part 2 15

Chapter 6: Don't Judge A Team By Its Cover 18

Chapter 7: My Fault 22

Chapter 8: Insecure Leaders 26

Chapter 9: Nip It In The Bud 31

Chapter 10: Sometimes The Bite Has To Be Bigger Than The Bark 32

Chapter 11: If That's The Way You Want It 34

Chapter 12: This Will Hurt Me More Than It Will Hurt You 35

Chapter 13: The One That Got Away 38

Chapter 14: A Few That Didn't Get Away 40

Chapter 15: Go To Rome 43

Chapter 16: Look At It This Way 44

Chapter 17: Perspective 47

Chapter 18: A Little Levity 48

Chapter 19: Pay Them Back 51

Chapter 20: Paying You Back 52

Chapter 21: The Shirt Off His Back...Literally 53

Chapter 22: I'll Show You 56

Chapter 23: Whether You Think You Can Or Can't, You Are Right 57

Chapter 24: Nice Job Coach! 59

Chapter 25: A Story For The Grandkids 62

Chapter 26: Insecure Leader #2 63

Chapter 27: You Treat Everyone Equally, But Not The Same 68

Chapter 28: Not My Cup Of Tea 70

Chapter 29: I've Fallen And I Can't Get Up…But I'm Still Pitching 74

Chapter 30: Tough Catch 76

Chapter 31: It's Not About You... It's About Me 79

Chapter 32: Music To The Ears: Part 3 82

Chapter 33: How You Are Dressed Is How You Will Be Treated 85

Chapter 34: Double Play 87

Chapter 35: Planted Not Buried 90

Chapter 36: Great Leaders, Great People 94

Chapter 37: Great Questions 97

Chapter 38: Two Great Leaders, My Mom And Dad 124

Testimonials 129

Acknowledgements 165

About Claudio 168

DEDICATION

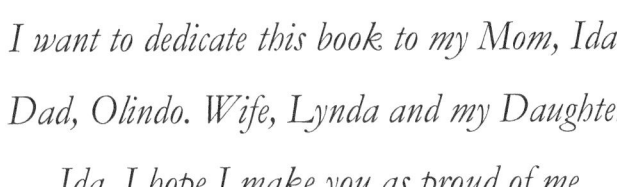

*I want to dedicate this book to my Mom, Ida.
Dad, Olindo. Wife, Lynda and my Daughter
Ida. I hope I make you as proud of me
as I am of all of you.*

INTRODUCTION

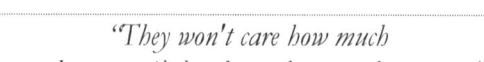

*"They won't care how much
you know until they know how much you care"*

It was a back and forth game. We were up, the other team came back. Then we scored 1 more to go ahead. The other team scored 2. Finally, we scored 3 to win the game. Our team went nuts! Hugging each other, laughing, high fives, coming to me hugging me and saying, "Congratulations Coach"! Or "We won this for you Coach!" It was not a playoff game; it was a regular season game. That is just the type of emotion my players had. I was drained as I am after all my games, but for some reason, this game was different. I remember sitting in front of my locker and I could not move. Just as I said totally drained. While I sat there, I started to think, "Why do my players treat me so well? Why do they listen to me the way they do? Why do they want to win for me?" I kept thinking of those questions and these answers jumped out at me—I am approachable, and I care.

Hello everyone, my name is Claudio Reilsono. I am the Head Baseball Coach at Carnegie Mellon University as well as the General Manger/Professional Baseball Scout for the Global Scouting Bureau. As of this writing, I have been coaching or scouting baseball for 37 years. I am 55 years old which means I started coaching right out of high school at the age of 18. Teams I have led have won 1 Collegiate Championship and 2 Conference Titles. More of my resume' in the back.

I am writing this book as if I am speaking to you. It will come from "The Heart up, not the Neck up" ...How I lead my players/teams. I work in both college baseball and professional baseball. I have coached some of the most amazing and wonderful people. They have played their hearts out for me. Many of them have become friends, some even brothers. I have been asked to be in their weddings, thought enough of to be (sadly) pall bearer for funerals, my players call me to meet their girlfriends and possible wife. They send me pictures of their newborn babies. I have gone golfing, fishing, dinners, watched World Series games with them. Many while they were playing for me.

What I will talk about in this book is how I was able to build and maintain a very special relationship with my players. And at the same time, lead them. Does this mean every single player was crazy about me? Of course not. I will mention that as well. But as you will read, many have incredibly positive things to say about me that I will include at the end of the book. I will share stories with you. Some dealing directly with me, or coaches I have worked under, admire or coached against. A lot of times I will not mention a particular school or coach because I am not here to embarrass anyone. I am here to help YOU become a better Coach, a better Leader by being better at developing relationships with your players or employees. Nor am I here to paint a picture of how wonderful I am and how others are not so. Once again, I just want to give you examples of what to do and what not to do. I may have a story pop in my head, I will write it down for you. I am not looking to do this in any order. Before each game and during, I will tell my team to "Huddle up". That is for adjustments, motivation, verbal notes. I will include as its own section throughout the book.

Again, my goal is to help you become a better leader. Doesn't matter what sport, or business you are the head of, or what age. This is not about X's & O's. It's about "Leading from the Heart up, Not the Neck up" I will use that phrase many times. My Mom Ida Reilsono used to say, "Claudio, never speak from the Neck up. Always speak from the Heart up. Never do anything from the Neck up. Always from the Heart Up" What does this mean? Don't be fake. Care. Be passionate. Give it your entire heart & soul.

After reading the opening you might think this book is going to be a sappy, "Love everyone and they will love you back" type book. Not really. But you will read about a lot of "Do's and Don'ts". How to treat people. Then how to lead them. Let's start with a few stories of don'ts.

FORWARD

Starting with GSB nearing 20 years ago, Claudio was persistent in his desire to be more (maybe even relentless) in his pursuit to help players in the game of baseball. Claudio exemplifies overcoming obstacles and remaining focused on helping others through his work in the game. Whether it be his college players at Carnegie Mellon or the hundreds of players he has assisted in advancement with Global Scouting Bureau, Claudio puts his wealth of knowledge and his whole heart into each and every player that crosses his path.

Although his passion and love of the game of baseball is great, his true strength and greatest quality in my humble opinion is his love of family. Rarely do people get to meet such a genuine individual which takes on the responsibility of father, husband, son, coach, mentor and friend with such pride.

Claudio pours his heart into all he does, and this book is an example of such. Even when things were tough, Claudio has always found ways to exemplify true leadership and the highest level of character. It is a privilege and honor to not only work with Claudio, but to now call him "a friend". All of us at GSB are very proud of him and having known his Father….he and his Mother are as well.

James L. Gamble
Owner of the Global Scouting Bureau
Co-Author of "IT'S MY TIME"

Chapter 1

THE COLD SHOULDER

We were in a bus waiting for the rest of the team to get on so we could go back home. One of our players who had not pitched at all during the season due to a shoulder injury comes up to me and says "Coach, my arm feels great. I am ready to play" This young man came to practice every day. Worked out with the team and by himself... everyday. Would come to the 2 a day practices we had as well. He ran, lifted weights, would measure how far and how fast he could throw the ball. Again, worked his tail off. He had one goal in mind. To pitch for us before he graduated. He wanted to help our team.

He approached me with such pride and confidence. I was so happy for him. So I told him "That is so great. I am very proud of you, and to be honest, we need pitching like crazy! I would go and tell the Head Coach". The Head Coach was sitting on the right side of the bus, first seat reading a newspaper. Had his glasses at the tip of his nose. I remember it like it was yesterday. So the Pitcher walks up to him and says "Coach, I am ready to help this team. I can pitch!" The Head Coach doesn't even look away for the paper. He said, "I am busy now, come talk to me on Monday!" Wow. It's a good thing the Head Coach was not talking to the Bus tires, because the tires would have deflated...just like the young man was.

He did end up pitching for us and doing well. But was that comment and attitude necessary? I don't think so.

Me and Sammer Kolluri. Never a bad time to communicate.
(Photo courtesy of the author)

Chapter 2

THE WRONG DOOR

Another time, (Same Coach) I was in his office and we were doing some work. One of our players knocks on the door comes in and asks the Head Coach if he could talk to him for a minute. He said "Coach, there is this girl I like and I would like to ask her out. To be honest, I have never asked a girl out before and really am having a very hard time with this. I am terrified to ask her out. Is there any advice you can give me on this The Coach very firmly said "My door says Head Baseball Coach, not Relationship Coach!" The player really didn't know what to say. Nor did I. As the player was heading out the door, the Coach said, "In Some cultures the symbol for failure is the same as success" Now what the Hell did that pertain to this young man I do not know. But that's what happened.

HUDDLE UP

What would it have taken for this "Coach" to be positive/help these 2 players? How hard would it have been to tell the first Pitcher, "Hey, I have seen you work every day. You never missed a practice. I am so proud of you. You will get some playing time this week. We will bring you in slowly. Again, proud of you and Thank you!" Or to the other player, "You know, I went through the same thing...many times. (Tell a story giving an example). Why would you want to be "Hard Ass" with them? How could you play for someone who didn't care for you and wasn't interested in what you were going through? He trusted you enough and thought enough of you to approach you with a problem and you gave him the "Cold shoulder"? Not what a good leader should do.

YOUR NOTES

Chapter 3

HE WAS THERE...
BUT HE WASN'T THERE

*Left to right Sammer Kolluri., Drew Himmelrich,
Cam Dively, Josh Solarek, Claudio Reilsono, Zac Etteonsohn,
Morgan Dively, Nick Halbedl, Eric Reeder.
(Photo courtesy of the author)*

A few "Do's" now. (I was the Head Coach) We were having a practice and one of my players was kind of going through the motions. He WAS at practice, but he WASN'T at practice. So I pulled him over and asked what was wrong. He said he was having problems with his girlfriend. So I simply told him "Leave. Go fix things up with your girlfriend." His eyes got as big as baseballs! I guess from shock number one, and from appreciation number two. He flew out of practice a lot faster than he did running in practice. That kid always gave me 100% but after that, he gave me 1000%!

Chapter 4

MUSIC TO THE EARS: PART 1

Another time, same team, 4 guys came up to me before practice and said "Coach, do you mind if we leave practice a little sooner today? Say around 6? We have tickets to a concert and it starts at 8." We started practice that day at 5:30 and done at 7. First off, these guys were good people who worked hard and played hard for us. So I told them, "If you leave here at 6, go home, get cleaned up, drive to the city, hit traffic it is going to be a hectic evening. All you will be doing is rushing around. I don't want that, nor do I want you to get into an accident. Go now. Get some extra reps in tomorrow." They couldn't believe I said that, but they were very appreciative. They deserved that from me. Those guys were always giving us/me what they had, but after that...they gave even more. You may ask, "How did the other players react to this?" Number one, they knew that these four players were good people and again, deserved respect and kindness. Number two they knew that if THEY worked hard, if THEY were good people that THEY would too be given such consideration from me.

Another thing, if I would have said no, they would have been upset with me, they would have had their minds on a game plan to make the concert on time, not practice. So again, they "Would" have been there but the "Wouldn't" have been there.

Chapter 5

MUSIC TO THE EARS: PART 2

That story was from 1993. The same thing happened in 2020. I had a player who was at every practice, worked hard, was a team leader in every sense of the word. He asked me if he could leave a bit early because he and some friends were going to a concert. It told him the same thing I said 27 years earlier, "Go ahead and go. Don't worry about practice for today. Get some extra time in tomorrow." He was grateful. But then something hit me. I did not want him to think that I let him miss practice because practice wasn't important. So I sent him a text explaining why I let him miss a day. "I just want to let you know that the reason why I was so quick in saying just miss a day of practice and go to the concert was not because practice isn't important, or this team isn't important. It's because you are important. You work hard and deserved my decision." We talked about it a little more the next day as well. This young man appreciated my actions and words and tried even harder for me/us.

HUDDLE UP

Coaches, Leaders have to understand, people who play for you, work for you look up to you. They are hoping that they can trust you, count on you and make them better. More successful. Happier. And let's face it, they want you to like them. Care for them. When you are cold or try to be a "Tough guy" type leader it doesn't work. You may see certain coaches on TV hollering at players or being very demonstrative and feel that those coaches may be a little rough on their players. But that is not it at all. They are passionate about what they do and who they are doing it with. Vince Lombardi, every coach (my age and older) studied Coach Lombardi. Was he tough? Yes, was he demanding? Yes. Did he holler at his guys? Yes, again...but did he care for those players? Was he there for them on the field and off? Did he try to not only make them better football players but better men? Yes, to all of the above. If you listen to interviews done by his Green Bay Packer football team, you will see quickly how much love they had/have for him. The reverence in which they speak of him. How he had major impact on their lives, to this day.

YOUR NOTES

Chapter 6

DON'T JUDGE
A TEAM BY ITS COVER

Anyone who knows me knows that I HATE being late for anything. If my flight leaves at 10am, I am at the airport at 6, 6:30. Nor do I like it when my players are late...really if anyone is late. Anyway, we were playing a team that had beaten us 3 years in a row. 3 years in a row by 1 run. They were a very good team, organized, great looking field, great overall facilities etc. So we are playing them on a Saturday. As always, I am there early, brought my wife Lynda and daughter Ida with me. It was a noon time start I like my players to be there about an hour and ten minutes prior to game. Well it is 11:25. (We have to drive to games ourselves in case you were wondering) and no team. I am in the dugout by myself. I could hear the fans laughing at us, and my wife and daughter heard fans saying things like, "This will be a quick game...if we play!" and "They must not have any respect for the Coach to be this late!" The opposing team finished very militaristic looking calisthenics, then had a great round of infield/outfield. Here I am by myself!! All of a sudden, I see my players pulling in. Some are half dressed, some have their shirts untucked, belts hanging and not buckled, and they come to me by two's and say

"Sorry coach, we hit traffic!" I said, "Great, hurry up and get dressed!!" Another couple of guys come and they say, "Coach we are so sorry, we stopped and got some takeout food and we hit traffic!" "Yeah terrific, go get ready!!" I barked. Well we were amusing the fans and the other team pretty good...Until we won the game, 8-0! After the game you could see the other coach hollering at his team (you could hear it too!) He was laying into them pretty good. My post game speech was, "You guys drive me nuts! But there is no team I'd rather have than you! Great job! Proud of you!" So as good as the other team looked prior to the game, as bad as we looked, (prior only) we won! Now, should the other coach have hollered at his group? No, I don't think so. They certainly tried hard, we just played with a little more heart and swagger. So as much as I hate being late, sometimes you just have to understand the situation.

HUDDLE UP

Don't be a hard liner. If a team, group or an individual is late, find out why and handle in accordingly. Or really any situation that is against the norm or what you what and expect, look into it. See why things happened the way they did. Another thing I want to mention really quick is, yes players your employees make mistakes. Help fix them but don't snap out on them because one day, you as a leader are going to make a mistake. If you are the type of Coach/Leader who gets on someone really hard after they make a mistake, and then one day you make one, don't be surprised if they get on you or look at you with a little smile and wink and are glad you got that taste of medicine.

YOUR NOTES

Chapter 7

MY FAULT

Case and point, we were involved in a game where we were down 8 runs. Couple of things were going on that day. If we win, it would have been the most wins ever for a CMU baseball team and it was my birthday. Well trust me when I tell you the guys were talking more about winning for my birthday than having the All-time wins mark at CMU. I wanted it for them, they wanted it for me. So we make this great, great comeback! We tie the game up! We were home team and it was the last inning. One more run and we win! So there was a timeout by the other team. We now have the game winning run standing on 2nd base. So I have something that you usually don't have in baseball as a coach, and that is time to think. Time to put scenario's in your head and know what you plan on doing next if this happen, if that happens etc... I said to myself, "If the ball is hit to left, left center or center field, send the runner home. The left fielder and centerfielder have below average arms. If it is hit to right center, probably send him home, if it is hit directly to the right fielder, DO NOT SEND HIM HOME! HE HAS A CANNON FOR AN ARM!!" Plus, I have the heart of my line up coming up. So here we are, made a great come back, last inning 2 outs. I have all the scenario's in my head, let's go! My hitter hits a line drive single directly to the right fielder. What do you think I did? Yep! I sent him. He was out by a mile. Damn. I messed up. Big time. Extra innings. As I walk towards our dugout on the 3rd base side I told my team "Hey guys, I am so sorry. I messed up. Get me out of this." They said, "We got you Coach! We will take care of things, don't worry!" I get emotional thinking about it now. 12 years later. Well, we lost. As is custom, after the game we line up down the foul line. I could not talk. I was bent over, hands on knees. Could not talk or look at my guys. They busted their tales to make this huge comeback, and I let the emotions get the best of me and blew it for the team. All I said was, I was sorry. They didn't lose the game I did. While I am still looking at the ground, I heard a voice say "No Coach, If I would have pitched better, we would have won. Sorry." Then another voice said, "If I would have gotten a hit with the bases loaded in the 7th inning, we would have won. My fault Coach" It kept going on, "My fault." "My bad." That was a tough loss, but I will never forget what my guys said and how they reacted after the game. Special group.

HUDDLE UP

If I would have been a hard ass with these guys, not approachable during the season, you know what they would have said? "Yeah, it was your fault!". They would have been glad I messed up! If you show that you care for them as people and as players, they will care back. If you are understanding of their mistakes, or whatever, they will be understanding to you when you mess up..and you will mess up. Simple.

YOUR NOTES

Chapter 8

INSECURE LEADERS

Without getting to deep into the stories here are a few things that a couple of "Leaders" did to me.

- ✪ Threw, let's just call it, "Fruit" at me during games.
- ✪ Made the transportation difficult to games. Tried to lose me as I was following him. (No GPS then!)
- ✪ Hired an assistant and took money out of my salary to pay him without me knowing.
- ✪ The more we won, the less he spoke to me. (The person who hired me)
- ✪ Gave us less and less time on the field to practice. From 2 ½ hours to 1 hour
- ✪ Asked me to meet in his office at 1. Didn't show up. Said he forgot. Waited for 3 hours. (A front office person in the Athletic Dept.)
- ✪ Would pretty much go against everything I would teach my players (A Head Coach)
- ✪ When other schools would inquire about me, said I was not a good coach.

- ✪ Removed players from team for "Violations" (A front office person in the Athletic Dept.)

I will tell this story. I had just gotten the Head Coaching job. The person who hired me would attend the games. So many of the moves I would make, steal sign, bunt, hit & run whatever, he would shake his head, sigh, or wave in disgust. I really wanted to impress him because I wanted him to bring me back as the Head Coach. So when he would show disgust, I quickly would change the call. Finally, my pitcher was not doing so great and he barks to me "Are you going to get him out of there or what??" So I open the gate to go on the field to take the pitcher out, take about 4 steps towards the mound and said "Hell with it" (Actually I said something else) "I am leaving him in there!" The pitcher finished the game and did great. On top of that we won. We went on a tear after that. I knew then and my team knew then it was MY Team.

So you may ask "Why did these people act this way? Treat you so disrespectfully? What role did you play in their behavior?" Who knows what goes through people's minds? But in my opinion, it was insecurities. I guess I was a threat. I should not have been. I was there to do my job, help the players, coaches win. Get better. I would never back stab anyone. Never tried to move in so I could get "The Big Seat" If I was Head Coach, I tried to make my team better on the field and off while appreciating the opportunity the person ahead of me gave me. I did not deserve the way I was treated. I was not the one with the problem. They were.

HUDDLE UP

Now back to me and my teams. Am I going to tell you that everything is wonderful and sweet with a Claudio Reilsono Coached team? Of course not. I am sure, out of the 37 years I have been coaching that there are a few (And I do mean a very few) who were not all that crazy about ME. And did I ever have to get mad at or punish a player?
For sure. Couple of examples..

YOUR NOTES

_____

_____

_____

_____

_____

_____

_____

_____

_____

_____

_____

_____

*On third base with Bryant Backus.
(Photo courtesy of the author)*

Chapter 9

NIP IT IN THE BUD

My very first year as a Head Coach. I was 23 and coaching at my old high school. I had been assistant for the past 5 years, now I am in the Big Seat. First day of practice. We were to be inside but it was nice out so I told the team, "It's warm, let's go outside on the field" Well, one of the players rolled his eyes, sighed loudly and said "Do we really have to go outside?" I snapped back in a loud voice, "No Al! (expletive) You can stay here in the gym by yourself or go the hell home. I really don't care" Right then and there everyone knew I was not going to put up with any attitudes. Never had another problem that year.

Chapter 10

SOMETIMES THE BITE HAS TO BE BIGGER THAN THE BARK

Huddle Up!!!! (Photo courtesy of the author)

Fast forward many years later, had a great player. I tried to help him be even greater, tried to get along with him. He was a little cold, standoffish, maybe even a little cocky. This one particular game he was pitching and as he was coming off of the field to the dugout I asked him if he was OK, if his arm was good and he got a little mouthy and that was it! I snapped on his ass pretty good. His eyes got as big as home plate! After I snapped on him in front of everyone for about 5 minutes, we NEVER had another problem. As a matter of fact, we are very close. Whenever he is in town, we always get together. When his kids are born, I am one of the first people he sends pictures to. Great young man doing great things.

Chapter 11

IF THAT'S THE WAY YOU WANT IT

I had a player when I was an assistant who just never warmed up to me. I would not say that he didn't listen to me, but there just was not a lot of interaction with us. His loyalties were to the Head Coach. He knew the Head Coach and I were not on good terms, so he chose sides. I understood that. How did I handle it? I knew no matter what I would say to this player he was not going to be receptive to it and on top of that, he would give me an attitude. If he continued to behave like that with me, I would have blown up. So, I just let him stay in his lane and I stayed in mine. If not, it would have not been a good situation. I accepted the situation as it was. You may ask, "But you are not coaching him? You are not making him better? And what about communicating with him?" All valid questions. I tried. He put up a wall. Remember, I did attempt to work with him and try to make him better. He just didn't want to hear it. So Again, I let him stay in his lane I stayed in mine. No incidents ever occurred.

Chapter 12

THIS WILL HURT ME MORE THAN IT WILL HURT YOU

Another time one of my players had his girlfriend coming into town. We had a doubleheader the day she was arriving. He said "Coach, I am going to have to miss tomorrow's game because my girlfriend is coming in." I said, "why don't you bring her to the game like everyone else does when they have a girlfriend that's visiting?" He just kind of shrugged and smiled. It was a big game that he was going to miss but that doesn't matter. It was a game. So I flat out told him, "I appreciate you telling me the truth, but if you do not come to the game, I am going to have to suspend you. It will hurt me to do it and it will hurt the team if you are not on the field, but I have to." He didn't come. He was suspended. We have never spoken about it since. He is a wonderful young man. Works hard. Great player. We get along great. Every time he sees me before practice or a game, he smiles, puts his arm around me and says, "Hello Coach" and we will talk about stocks, life, and yes, some baseball. At the end of the day, he did what he had to do. I did what I had to do. We have moved on. He graduated and he is now in our team Hall of Fame. (We are meeting for breakfast this week!)

HUDDLE UP

As I look back on my career, the players that I had a "negative moment" with were my best players. There are some coaches out there that seem to jump on the guys who don't play as much and let the ones who do play a lot go. I never got that. Whoever needs it gets it is my philosophy. I tell my team at the beginning of every year. "Do not do anything that will upset me. Do not disrespect me, your teammates, or the school. Give me everything you have. Care for the team. That's it" Another phrase I use not only with my team but with my family is:

"If we all pull the same rope at the same time in the same direction, for the same purpose we will get a special result" If you have a player/employee who is not doing this, the biggest and best thing to do is COMMUNICATE. You and this other person have to talk about why things are not good...on both ends. If that person is willing to communicate with you, then the chances for a successful, productive relationship are very, very high. They won't get away.

YOUR NOTES

Chapter 13

THE ONE THAT GOT AWAY

One player who was one of the very best players I ever coached did get away. This kid gave me and the team everything he had. He was all heart. Had a ton of talent. He would come to me during the game and say, "I'll pitch coach" or I'll catch coach" Always with a confident grin. He brought me to tears many, many times during and after games. We would have discussions about life, business many topics. I tried to be there for him when things were tough. He was so good that I thought that maybe, just maybe he could play Pro if given a shot. Well I tried hard to get him in. The Pro company I work for, Global Scouting Bureau tried. Nothing. Now we could have gotten him tryouts for sure...and maybe even sign him to Independent League baseball and for sure overseas, but he wanted drafted and that was not going to happen. We have not spoken since the MLB June draft a few years ago. Not sure why. Now it could be because I could not get him drafted. Also, when I was honored to win this particular award, I wanted him there. He was a huge, huge part of me getting that award. He didn't show. He said he thought it was on a different day. It hurt me that he didn't come. I was invited to his graduation party and I did not go due to a baseball camp I had to go to. Maybe he thought I was getting even. Who knows? Again, we have never spoken again. Now you may be saying, "Why don't YOU communicate with him?" Good point. I was hoping he would come back to the team for one more semester then we would resolve things, but it never happened. He is doing very well in business and I am happy for him. Although saddened that we are no longer friends. Very saddened. He got away. It would be nice if we connected again. Maybe our friendship would be stronger than it was before. I hope it happens.

Chapter 14

A FEW THAT DIDN'T GET AWAY

A player that didn't is Vince Kaplack. I coached Vinny my first year as a Head Coach (again, I was 23 and he was 17) Vinny was not, and still isn't close to many people but we hit it off. Vinny is not a friend, he is family. His entire family is my family. I also coached his brother Nick. Nick is family. (Both have gone on to have successful careers. Vinny was also an 11-time Champion Pro Wrestler, and Nick has won several Championships as a Baseball Coach in Ohio and both wonderful family men) Many of my players from CMU as well as my other jobs still keep in touch. They come to our games, banquets, they invite me to dinner go golfing. It's a great thing and it means so much to me.

HUDDLE UP

Wouldn't you rather have players or people who work for you like you? Want to be around you? I think the old saying "I don't care if they like me as long as they respect me!" Is out the window. Players, employees will go all the way TO the wall for you if they like OR respect you. Players, employees will go THROUGH a wall for you if they like AND respect you. Or like my Dad, Olindo used to say, "You will attract more bees with honey than you will mustard!"

YOUR NOTES

Chapter 15

GO TO ROME

One of my players calls me about 1 am. I see his name on my caller ID and start to worry. First thing I said was, "What's wrong?" "Coach, I really need to talk to you, but I can't do it now." I said, "Don't do this to me, tell me…what's wrong" "Tomorrow Coach, I just can't talk" So I am all worked up. Can't sleep. All these things are going through my mind as to what could be the problem. I am sure as you are reading this, you have several things in your mind as to what could have been the problem. I see him in the morning, he does not look good. So I ask, "What's going on" He says, "Coach I have an opportunity to study in Rome." So I said "AND????? What's the problem???" He said, "Coach, you and the team need me. I need the team." So after my heart slows up I simply told him that the team and I will still be here when he gets back. Go! This was a great opportunity for him…take it! He did. Did great in Italy and came back to our team. After graduation, he too became a member of our team Hall of Fame.

Chapter 16

LOOK AT IT THIS WAY

Another similar story is right before our first playoff game ever our Senior Captain said he needed to talk to me after the game. He was really down in the mouth. So again, I was worried. So after our playoff win, he comes to my hotel room and says (with tears in his eyes) "Coach, I don't want to leave the team, and I don't want to leave you. This team has been such a great experience for me." Man, that got to me. So after I wiped my tears and thanked him for his sentiment and words, I told him of the quote I read as you leave the iconic Hershey Park said by the legendary Dr. Seuss "Don't cry because it's over, smile because it happened"

HUDDLE UP

Again, if I was some sort of "tough guy" with these young men or made the baseball culture at CMU or any school I coached at bad they would have been glad to get away...especially from me. In other words, you yourself as a leader have to be a good person, understanding person and create a culture where your players/employees love it there. A place where they look forward to being, not leaving.

YOUR NOTES

Chapter 17

PERSPECTIVE

I tell my players all the time, "Be intense, but not tense" I had a freshman pitcher who had a great high school career on the mound for me. It was his first game for us. Well he walks the first 2 batters, hits the 3rd batter. I go to the mound and I see his right hand (while holding the ball) is shaking. So I asked "Are you OK? Are you hurt? "He said, "No coach, I am just real nervous" So let me back track, his father was a cancer Doctor. So I said to him, "Nervous?? You are playing baseball. Beautiful day, what's there to be nervous about? The people who go see your Dad should be nervous. They have something to worry about, not you." I said all of this on the mound. No strategy or covering up my mouth when I am speaking (By the way, I hate that!) I just wanted to put things in perspective for him. How did he do? Well, not too good. He didn't last through the next inning. BUT, while he was getting hit pretty hard, at least he was relaxed and put it in perspective! (Hey, not all stories are going to end great!!)

Chapter 18

A LITTLE LEVITY

Sometimes I will have a player who might be struggling. He will come up with bases loaded or in scoring position. A real pressure situation. I will call timeout, ask the player to come over to me. I will tell him, "I am going to pinch hit for you, OK? I have done this numerous times and each time the player puts his head down. Obviously very disappointed begins to walk towards the dugout... Then I will tell him, "I am kidding!! I know you will come up big! You are due. I WANT you to be the guy who is up now! Go get 'em!" Sometimes it works, sometimes it doesn't but I am trying to take some pressure off while showing them that I believe in them.

HUDDLE UP

I want to win and I want to win badly! But, you have to put things in perspective. I always tell my teams, "While you are here on the field, give me everything you have and make this important. As soon as the game is over, you move on to your

"real life" and to what is really important. Perspective.

YOUR NOTES

Chapter 19

PAY THEM BACK

This year, we had a doubleheader. The first game was at the opposing colleges field on campus, the 2nd game was to be played at night at a really nice minor league ballpark. So I told my senior pitcher (who I usually start him game 1 on doubleheaders) that I was going to start him game 2 because I wanted him to have the experience of pitching at a beautiful minor league ballpark. His eyes lit up. He was very appreciative. This young man did not play when he first joined the team. He never once complained or was a pain. He was a very quiet young man. All he did was put his head down and work. He went after it. He not only did he become our best player, a player I could count on, but he was one of our team leaders.

Chapter 20

PAYING YOU BACK

Another time, we had a game that if we win, we go to the Championships. I started a pitcher who I knew since he was a kid. Someone who came to the college because of me. Even though he pitched briefly during the season due to arm problems, I had a hunch he would go out there and pitch his heart out...at the risk of sounding arrogant about it, he would pitch his heart out for me. I was criticized for starting someone who was not 100% and who had not pitched much during the year. But again, I just knew he would give me all he had, and then some. Well long story short, we won the game 11-0, and he pitched a complete game 1 hitter! I kept asking him during the game if he was OK, his answer was always "Hell Yeah! I am good!" After we won, I told him how proud I was of him and he simply said, "I appreciate you believing in me. I appreciate what you have done for me. There was no way I was letting you down!"

Chapter 21

THE SHIRT OFF HIS BACK...LITERALLY

Another one of my players who was kind enough to write a testimonial for me is Sameer Kolluri. At our team awards banquet where Sameer was one of the Hall of Fame inductees, his father came up to me. "Coach, Sameer has said so may wonderful things about you how you have helped him on the field but more importantly off the field. I cannot thank you enough." Well obviously, that meant the world to me. So, I went on to tell him how wonderful it was to coach Sameer and I am going to miss coaching him but I know we will remain friends. Then I proceeded to say, "You know Mr. Kolluri, as soon as you walked into this room, I noticed your beautiful yellow Polo pullover!" He didn't say a word. He stepped back away from me and took it off and said, "here you go coach...it's yours!" I said, "No, No I was just saying how beautiful it was, you don't have to do that!" Then Mr. Kolluri simply said, "Coach, this is the least I can do for you after what you have done for us". I was so touched. Then I found out he had recently bought a BMW. I should have told him how beautiful the car was!!!!!

HUDDLE UP

So believe in your people. Show appreciation for your people. When you do, I truly feel you will not only get their best, but several levels more. You try to be a plus and do something special for them…they will appreciate it and try to do something special for you.

YOUR NOTES

Chapter 22

I'LL SHOW YOU

This next story happened to me as a player. In 1983 me along with 2 of my friends went to see the new American Legion coach. There were a few other guys from the team there as well. So the coach starts to talk about a line up. Starts to say this guy is going to do great here, that guy will be super over there, this player will be an All-Star. Then he looked at me and said "Claudio, I don't know if I am going to be able to use you." You have to understand, I was the best player on all my teams...by far and now I might not even make the team?? He made me feel like I was not even there. I did hurt my Achilles the season past, but I was ready. I had worked very hard to make sure I could be back on the field and contribute...big time. So I asked him "Coach, when is the All-Star game this year?" He said "July 3" "OK, well, I promise you I will be on the All-Star team. No doubt. Write it down!" Well of course I made the All-Star team. I led our team in all offensive categories as well as leading the team in assists. He first treated me like a nothing. That hurt me. So I wanted to show him...and I did.

Chapter 23

WHETHER YOU THINK YOU CAN OR CAN'T, YOU ARE RIGHT

I coached a young man, Zac, (who wrote me a great testimonial for this book) who was just the best person you could ever meet. (I have coached a ton of people like that) Anyway Zac is about 6'6 always had a smile on his face, again, just as nice as anyone could be. And on top of that watching him play when he first got on the field, you could see that he was special. He had a beautiful swing (he was a lefty) great hands as a first basemen. In my opinion, he had pro ability. But his freshman year, the numbers didn't show that. He worked hard, but things didn't go the way we wanted. He was hitting I think in the .200's. So I took him aside and simply said to him, "Zac, I know talent when I see it. I trust my eyes more than anyone. You have big time ability and on top of that you are a great person. I truly think you have a .500 swing in you. But it doesn't matter what I think. YOU have to think this. YOU have to know it!" So then I said the great and true quote from the Founder of the Ford Motor Company, Henry Ford, "Whether you think you can, or whether you think you can't, you are right". I would say this to Zac just about every game. Well, I was wrong about Zac. I said he had a .500 swing in him. He went on to hit .700!! He went crazy! I was so happy for him. His smile got even bigger...and so did mine.

Chapter 24

NICE JOB COACH!

Grateful to be living my dream! (Photo Courtesy of the author)

As I have mentioned before, when leading a team, it is incredibly important to show belief in them. Trust them. One time (I was an assistant) we lost a game that we should have won and the team was down. Our next game was against a very big-name school and they were just on a much higher level than us. As I looked at their schedule, I saw that they had a weekend series against their biggest rival! They were rivals in baseball, basketball and especially football. So the next day on our way to their field, in small groups I told our team, "They have a big weekend of games coming up and I really think they are going to overlook us. This is a great chance to sneak up on them and pull out a win. It would make big news, and really be a boost to our program." Well that message floated from one group, to another, to another. When we left our campus, we were not so sure we were going to make it past the 10-run mercy rule. By the time we got there, we thought we were going to win! The guys had a different look, about them. Well as we pulled up to the field, the Head Coach said "We know we are going to lose today but let's learn from this loss. Let's try some different things to see how they go. At least when we lose, we can get something out of it." Nice. We came out hot. By the 3rd inning we were up 3-1. The team was focused and hungry. Then the Head Coach decided to "Try different things". Steal a base when the runner was not fast. A hit and run at the wrong time and I think, if memory serves, we tried a squeeze play with 2 outs. Then on top of all of that, he took our regular right fielder and moved him to catcher in the middle of the game. Did the same thing with our shortstop, moving him to left field. We lost and lost big. It was a circus. The team was again deflated. No one said a word on the way back to campus.

Chapter 25

A STORY FOR THE GRANDKIDS

A few seasons ago, we had a game against the first-place team. We were down players so this made it tougher. My guys knew that I believed in them. They believed in themselves. We won game 1. Game 2, the next day we were down early, something like 11-0. My guys kept fighting. Then I heard one of my players, Tyler Scanlon say "Let's keep at it, we win this then we have something we can tell our grand kids about!" That's the attitude I always talk about! We are up 10 score 11. Down 10 score 11. Keep after it. I never stopped believing we could win. Nor did they. Did we win the game? No, but we tried like crazy and were a better team and people for the effort. We can still tell our grand kids about it.

Chapter 26

INSECURE LEADER №2

I was assistant coach coaching first base. The Head Coach said to me, "When a runner gets on first, pretend that you are the runner and lead off of first. Then jump like you are stealing a base. This way he will think you are the runner" Now I knew this Coach couldn't be that stupid. (He was though) but he wanted to embarrass me. Why? Insecurities. So here I am n first base pretending to lead and then jump towards second base. I felt stupid. People in the stands were laughing at me. I knew it. The Head Coach knew it. I did what I was told because this was a good job/opportunity for me. But I kept hearing the laughter and remarks so I said "To hell with this, I am not going to keep making an ass out of myself" so I told the Coach I am not doing that anymore. In my heart and mind I was done! I was going to quit. So after the game, we went to a college close by to change, and get ready for our next game. I was going to cuss the coach out and quit. So as I am waiting for him, my girlfriend at the time, Lynda who is now my wife came to see me off. I told her I was going to snap on the coach then quit. So wait here to take me home. She tried to convince me not to do this, but I was going to no matter what. While

I was waiting, I kept thinking of my Mom and Dad. I promised them both that no matter what I would never stop on our dream of me working in pro baseball. Where I was a good little step in that direction. So I didn't quit. I stayed on. I was going to at least finish the year with this guy. It was hard because he continued to try to embarrass me. Finally, one day he called and said he was not going to bring me back as an assistant. I told him he beat me to the punch and I didn't think it was a good idea for me to come back for several reasons. I felt like a ton of bricks were off of my shoulders! After all these years, revisiting that time, I STILL am upset and sick by the way he treated me. I have nothing good to say about this guy. Don't YOU be that way. Don't let a player or an employee say that you made them sick. That you embarrassed them. That you stripped them of their confidence. Stripped them of their hope. Don't be like THAT guy. PLEASE don't. Oh yeah, 2 more stories on this guy. Before a practice I was supposed to work with the hitters, as I am speaking to them he flips me the keys to his car and says, "Go get air for the wheelbarrow at the gas station". Like I was some ass. Another time we were going on a road trip. He reads a list of the names who was going to go. Which was the entire roster...except me. Several of the players asked, "You didn't mention Coach Claudio's name" He just said "He is not going" I felt about as low as you could feel as a coach. He could have told me privately, but he wanted to embarrass me. Again, you may ask "What did you do to this guy for him to treat you like this"? 1000 % honest opinion here. He was jealous that I was a much, much better coach and communicator than him. I was a threat to him. So he wanted to sink me. Strip me of any confidence I had in myself. Well I am embarrassed to say it worked. I let him. It took me a while to get it all back. Again, Do not do this to anyone. Again, I was an assistant. I would never ever back stab the Head Coach to replace him, look better than him or anything like that. I knew my boundaries and respected them. I was not the one with the problem. He was. He was not a good leader. Do not be like him. But I knew with all my heart that I was going to show him! I was going to get to where I wanted to go in spite of him. He was NOT going to make the job I had with him be my last stop!

HUDDLE UP

You should never treat your players/employees like they do not matter. Like they have no shot at being an important cog on your team. There is never a need to embarrass someone. You want your people to play hard for you, work hard for you, not in spite of or against you or have no heart for their work and efforts. It is very draining. It will create a bad culture. Yes, that coach motivated me, but if he would have been positive with me, or attempted to help me, it would have meant a lot and I would have gone after it with a different mindset. (Like Zac did) I would have done it out of appreciation, as well as to show them they were right in trusting me, right in having me on their staff. Yes, I went at it hard to prove him wrong, but it would have been a more pleasant success story if they were different. One like, "Thanks Coach for your help and belief in me" instead of, "I'll show you!" Always believe in your teams and people! Even if you don't think you have a chance for the win, for the successful deal or contract, show that you believe in them, show that you are confident in them! Make them feel that you have a shot! Who knows what can happen!! Again, "Whether you think you can or whether you think you can't, you are right"

Believe in your team. Be a plus in their lives, not a negative.

YOUR NOTES

_____

_____

_____

_____

_____

_____

_____

_____

_____

_____

_____

Chapter 27

YOU TREAT EVERYONE EQUALLY, BUT NOT THE SAME

When I coach, I am very intense. I give it everything I have. I really Coach during a game. It's just how I am. I am all wound up. Well one time, we were down and one of my players, Dan said something to me and I pretty much snapped at him. I will never ever forget the look on his face. He froze and was in shock. I hurt him. I hurt his feelings. Dan and I had (and still have) a great relationship. He did not expect me to snap at him like that. I felt awful. Some guys you can get on and they are fine. No relationship damage, no shock no nothing. The message gets through and it's all done after the game. Well Dan was more sensitive. I knew that too. But I behaved the way I did anyway. So when we were back in the dugout I simply apologized to him and just told him that I was so wound up and upset that we were not playing well and he happened to get it the way. He was great about it and it was never brought up again. That was about 7 years ago, Dan and I just had lunch about a month ago. We met because I wanted to tell him he was being inducted into our CMU baseball Hall of Fame. His face froze again, but this time with appreciation. I made a mistake. So will you. As a Coach, as a person who is running a company...as a parent. If you do make a mistake, fix it! Simple! Apologize, explain why you did and said what you said, say you are sorry and move on!

Chapter 28

NOT MY CUP OF TEA

There was a former boxing Champion who is a very good friend of mine. He is a wonderful person, highly intelligent person, and I guess you would say an easy-going guy. Now, obviously when fighting he can knock down a wall but all in all his personality is being a rather calm person. He had a trainer that was an in your face type of guy. Hollering at you, belittling you, then try to build you back up. Well, this trainer was not for my friend. He did not respond well to being hollered at, criticized, embarrassed. He felt his career in the ring was not only being stunted, but declining, so he fired the trainer. Now this trainer is considered one of the best, a Hall of Farmer BUT he just wasn't a good fit for my friend. Who again, went on to be a celebrated Champion after firing this trainer. So, what am I saying? Yes, the trainer is a great trainer BUT not for the type of person my friend needed or wanted. Some players or employees will thrive on someone hollering at them or getting on them. Some will just not like it and put up a wall or turn away from that type of action. So yes, be yourself but at the same time, see what type of person your player or employee will be attracted to. What type of Leader they will follow, not distance themselves from.

HUDDLE UP

I have been lucky to coach great people and great teams. But is every day perfect? Is every player perfect or great every day? Of course not. You can't have big ears and eyes. Now of course I am not saying to let a player or an employee disrespect you, but if possible, live by these great words by Hall of Fame basketball Coach Chuck Daly. He was asked one time how he was able to Coach such a "Different" group of players like the "Bad Boys" Detroit Pistons Championship teams. He simply said. "Bad hearing lousy eye site and a terrible memory" Keep those words in your pocket.

AM I saying to just let everything go...do what you want guys? Everything is fine. That's OK, don't worry about it? Of course not. I say this next line all the time. Don't just hear me saying it to you. Listen to it. You have to make adjustments in life! If it is 16 degrees outside in February and you saw someone wearing shorts outside, wouldn't he look dumb? Or if it was 86 degrees outside, muggy and you saw someone where long sweatpants and a sweatshirt, with a ski cap. Wouldn't like to look dumb? So I say, when it's cold, put on a jacket. When it's warm, throw on some shorts. MAKE THE NESSECARY ADJUSTMENTS! Know your players/employees. Know if you can raise your voice at this one or have to be calmer with that one. Everyone is motivated by different things and by different ways. You treat everyone equally, but not the same.

Some people might read this and say, "I don't want to be Buddy-Buddy with anyone! "Or the old phrase, "I don't care if they Like me they better respect me." "If I am too nice, they will take advantage of my kindness". I get all of that. I am not asking you to be "Buddy-Buddy. Just treat people right and care. I truly believe if you do that, they will NOT take advantage of your kindness. They will respect you, but they will also like you. And if they do try to take advantage of you, if they do not respect or like you, then you have to handle it and quick by either communicating with them or just get rid of them.

Some other events happened to be on my Birthday that I would like to share with you... One evening we were having practice then all of a sudden, I look around and we are missing 4 players. Where did they disappear to? They went and got me a birthday cake. Another time after a game, the other team was fighting with the coach for whatever reason. Again, it was my Birthday and after our win the guys presented me with a Birthday cookie that looked like a baseball. I am an emotional guy to begin with, but when they gave me the cake and sang to me! I was done. Corny, maybe but to me it shows what a great group I have…and have had. But if they couldn't stand me, would they have done this for me? You tell me.

YOUR NOTES

Chapter 29

I'VE FALLEN AND I CAN'T GET UP...BUT I'M STILL PITCHING

Earlier I mentioned Rainer Nunez. This one year I had no catcher. Not one! I asked Rainer to be the guy because #1, I knew he was a good enough athlete to pull it off. #2 I knew he was tough enough to do it and #3 he never says no to me! Well this one weekend I wanted him to pitch. I wanted him to pitch in this particular Ball Park, Pullman Park. It was a New York Yankee minor league ballpark many, many years ago and Rainer is a huge Yankee fan so I wanted to do this for him because of all he has done for me and the team. I get a text from Rainer late Saturday night...I mean late! His said "Coach, I fell down some steps, and I hurt my foot" So I called him. I said "How did you fall and when? Are you ok?" He said, "Just like 1 minute ago. I just fell and yeah, I'll be able to pitch tomorrow". He actually sent me a text from the bottom of the steps BEFORE he called anyone else or did anything about his foot! Why? Why did he not blink when I asked him to play a position he never played before? In my mind it's because he cared for me. I was important to him. That meant more to me than I can say.

So the story should go that Rainer went out and pitched a 3-hitter and we won the game right? Well no that's not what happened. He broke a bone, tore some ligaments. He needed major surgery. He did come to the game though...crutches and all. I was crushed because I could never coach him again. But the fact that he cared enough to call me when he did is something I will never forget.

Chapter 30

TOUGH CATCH

We were playing game #1 of a playoff game and I had to make a very tough decision. Which catcher do I start? Cam, who caught every game, every inning for me that past couple of years, and did an excellent job, or Josh who joined our team, played catcher this way I could give Cam a break from behind the plate, put Cam in the outfield or use him as the designated hitter. Well Josh was just great! Both on offense and defense. Now as we were moving closer to playoff time, I knew I had to make a very tough choice between 2 catchers but more importantly 2 great people. I owed it to the team to play who I thought would help us out the most. It was Josh. Okay; I made the tough decision. Great. Now I had to talk to Cam. So, I called him over at the field, about an hour prior to the game! Talk about last minute decisions! I would suggest you not wait so long to make a major decision like this, but I did. So, I take Cam aside and said, "Cam, I appreciate all you have done for me and this team. You are a huge reason that we are here playing in the playoffs. But I must make a tough move. I am going to start Josh behind the plate. (Cam was not going to play at all because my outfield was set and my pitcher could hit) I got choked up. Cam is, and I can say this about a ton of my players, the type of young man you want your daughter to marry. You know what Cam said? "No problem Coach! Josh is doing a great job and we need him in there" That's it! He then put HIS arm around ME and said, "Don't worry Coach, I am sure there will be opportunities for me to contribute" I get misty eyed thinking about this. Then I went to talk to Mr. & Mrs. Dively, Cam's parents. I told them about my move and Mrs. Dively simply smiled and Mr. Dively "Okay, well that's fine. You are the Coach. Thanks for talking with us but you didn't have to" I can see where Cam got his class. So we went on a nice run in the playoffs, Josh did great and Cam did contribute so it all worked out. I truly believe that if I had been, I will just come out and say it, "An ass of a Coach" or one that was not liked or respected by his players this may not have gone off so smooth. Not to say that Cam would have said or done anything negative, but I think the fact that he knows how much I cared for him made it a bit easier to handle it the way he did.

HUDDLE UP

All of these stories prove that if you "Lead from the Heart up, not the Neck up." as well as the other common theme to the book, "They won't care what you know until they know that you care", you will have success with your team, employees and family. Simple.

YOUR NOTES

Chapter 31

IT'S NOT ABOUT YOU... IT'S ABOUT ME

I do a lot of baseball training. Camps, clinics and private lessons. Primarily on hitting. So I was recommended to this young lady for hitting instruction. She was about 4'9 thin build about 13 years old, good athlete. Again, she was not hitting well. More specifically, having a hard time making contact and when she did she would pop up. So since I have never seen her hit before, I wanted to see her in the batting cage to see what she was doing well, and not so well. She was stepping way too early, and every swing she took she was uppercutting. Not to go into a hitting lesson, (again, another book!) but I would NEVER and have NEVER taught anyone to bat like this, especially a girl who was built the way she was. Also, this girl could run and run fast so why would you want her to hit the ball in the air? Plus, she was not a power hitter that was going to hit any homeruns! She was really frustrated and down. Her mom was very upset as well. Without going into a lot of hitting details, I turned this girl into what should was and that was a line drive hitter who made consistent contact. It got to the point where this little girl was hitting 80 MPH pitches in a batting cage! (And it is harder to hit off of a machine than a real pitcher) She was crushing the ball! So much so that boys her age to adult players were watching her and admiring her swing. She was not only pounding the ball, but she was confident and most important, she was enjoying the game again. Well now it was time to go to practice for the first time since her "new approach to hitting". The coach told her he didn't like what he saw and wanted her to go back to the old way even though this new approach was working and people were commending her for her success in practice. So she went back, failed again, and was miserable. So the mom asked me to call the coach and tell him how well she was doing with me and how good she can be. I said that I never like to tell another coach what to do with his team. She really pleaded with me so I called. Told him how much she improved and why she was doing so much better. He very simply said "I have been a softball coach for a lot of years. She either bats the way I tell her too or she does not play. She has to swing my way!" SO, I didn't want to get into it with him, I did not want to get into a battle of wits with an unarmed person, so I let it go. Listen to what he did next…He did change her again. From and small girl who he wanted homeruns from, to a left-handed slap hitter (She was right-handed). This girl could have been a big-time hitter. With her ability to hit line drive shots and fly she could have been big time. But no, he wanted her to do things "His way" She did, and she didn't do well. As a matter for fact she was told not to have me as her hitting coach or she would not play on that team. I have no idea what ever happened to her. So it was not about helping the player be better. It was not about providing a positive culture for this player or any player. It was about HIM the coach and getting HIS way out there.

Chapter 32

MUSIC TO THE EARS: PART 3

There was a singer who had huge success in his genre, but he decided he wanted to jump into another genre. He hired and brought in the best of the best to assist him with this album. The best musicians, the best singers. He wanted this to be a big-time project. So as he started the process, all of these great and successful musicians and singers were giving him advice. "Do it this way". "Try this". "Let's add this". The singer's head was spinning. He was trying to be respectful, but he knew how he wanted this album to sound and all they had to do was their job. Sing, sing backup or play your instrument. So after days and nights of hearing all the advice, the singer saw that he was getting nowhere. He called a late-night meeting and simply said, "I respect all of you as people and musicians or else you wouldn't be here. But I know exactly how I want this to sound so although I appreciate your input, we are going to do it this way. Thank you." The album was done in 4 days and did great in sales. The singer was right.

HUDDLE UP

So what am I saying? Am I saying two different things here? The first story, "It's not about you, it's about me" was about a coach who did not know what he was doing. About a coach who was on an ego trip. About a coach who was arrogant. It was proven that he was wrong. Do not be like that guy. The second story, "Music to the ears Part 3" The singer was a huge success prior to this project. Knew what he was doing, and he was proven right. What he was saying was making sense. So what am I telling you? It is not about you. I have been saying this throughout the book. Do all you can to help and make it a great, positive culture. If what you are teaching or asking your people to do is not working, fix it. Try something else. Maybe see what your team members have to say about it. Whatever works, let's do it. Or, if you are good at what you do, have a track record of success and you have a bunch of people in your ear telling you to do this, or that, politely tell them that you know exactly what to do and how to do it. You have an end in mind and how to get there. Have success with it, and everyone will see that you were right. Stick to your beliefs.

YOUR NOTES

Chapter 33

HOW YOU ARE DRESSED IS HOW YOU WILL BE TREATED

I used to see this one coach that never looked the part. He looked disheveled. Never cared how he looked. Uniform pants were always wrinkled, his hat was always misshaped, and he wore the worst looking baseball shoes too. When he came to games, his car was always dirty. I was told he was like this off the field too. When your players or employees see this, right away they will put a label on you. My Mom Ida used to tell me all the time, "How you are dressed is how you will be treated". She was right. If you look bad, players/employees will not have confidence in you, they will not have as much respect for you as they should. You want to exude confidence. Imagine going to a surgeon and his desk is a mess, he looks awful, would you want that person taking care of you? What would you think of that person? If you look bad, your players or employees may even feel that how they look isn't important because you are not too concerned about the way you look so they too will look bad. Now you might be saying this, "Claudio, you told a story a few chapters ago about your team coming to a game late, not all the way dressed, while the other team looked good and you still beat them." That's true, but that was because our guys were running late. They always looked good. Something just hit me as I am writing this. In all my years as a Head Coach I do not remember having to tell my players to look better. I think they know by how I try to look; they feel they should do the same thing.

Chapter 34

DOUBLE PLAY

I have to share this with you. My first year as Head Coach at Carnegie Mellon University I had a player that was always late. Late to practice, late to games. Now you have to understand, CMU is a very demanding school scholastically and my guys are up all night doing work so I am very understanding about that. But this young man was taking it a little too far. So in all honesty I thought that maybe, just maybe he was testing the new coach. Well I was not going to have it. I told him in a pretty stern way that this was the last day that he was going to be late for practice! That's it! No more excuses. No more reasons for being late! Nothing! He said he was sorry then simply promised that he would not be late again.

The very next day we had an away game and we were all going to meet at 8am in the gym to get on the bus. This young man got there before me and I got there at 6:45 am! He was dressed and ready to go. I told him thank you, he smiled and that was it. Then about 20 minutes later I see him in the door way dressed in a polo shirt, jeans and flip flops! I lost it!!! I said to myself, "He gets here before me to show me he is going to be on time, THEN he gets undressed to make me look like a fool?? No way. So I snap! I told him in no certain terms that I was not the guy to disrespect! I went on and on. He was about 6'4, thin, glasses, and while I am hollering at him, he looks at me with no expression on his face at all! Blank!! So as I am getting madder, for whatever reason I look to my left and there was my player dressed in his uniform! He had an exact twin! The whole team got a huge laugh at my expense and I apologized to the brother.

SO, A MINI HUDDLE UP

Make sure you are hollering at the right guy!!

YOUR NOTES

Chapter 35

PLANTED NOT BURIED

It was our first game of the 2015 season, and we were playing a very good ball club. It was a non-conference game but that never matters to me, I want to win every game. Not only did we lose, but we lost by the 10-run mercy rule. (Down by 10 after 5 innings) We did nothing right. We didn't hit. We didn't field well. Pitching was not there at all. I noticed our team was upset, embarrassed and I think they felt that this was going to be a long, losing season. After the game I simply told them "This is not the end of the world. This could be something that jump starts us to big things. It's our choice. We are not buried...we are planted. Again, it's our choice how we handle this. Now we know what we have to work on." Some coaches like to make their players do sprints to punish them, I guess. Some coaches I have seen would have snapped and yelled at the team. The only time I would do that as a team is if the team was not taking our game seriously, not caring, being disrespectful to me. Then the whole team would hear about it but that was not the case. So I say this to you- "Instead of punishing them, fix them." Simple. I also remember as I was leaving the field one of the parents came up to me and said,

"Coach, I hate to say it but you really have your work cut out for you this season." I said, what I always say, "We will be OK. We will work it out." I heard other fans saying things, the opposing team was pretty much laughing at us. Our first practice after a game I always go to each player individually and talk about what they did right and not so right. We all kept working to get better. Me included. Well that group went on to win the Conference Championship!

HUDDLE UP

If your team or organization does not get off to a good start, don't panic and make sure your team does not panic. Believe in your group, let them know that you believe in them. Work on what needs to be worked on. If people are saying that it doesn't look good or you are not going to succeed, remember this story:

The farmer was looking for his favorite old donkey. He looked and looked but could not find it. Then he sees that somehow the old donkey fell into a water well. He tried and tried to get him out but he just couldn't. So he decided to bury the donkey in the well so he began to throw dirt on it. After every shovel full of dirt, the donkey shook it off. More dirt hit him, the more he shook it off. It got to the point that so much dirt fell on the donkey, and so much dirt was shaken off that he stepped on the dirt and used it to climb out of the well! Lesson: Use negativity to motivate you. To make you climb higher. Not bury you. I look back at some of the things that happened to me in my life or career. I could have let it bury me. Some of the bad treatment I received from some of the people I worked for, some family members who were not supportive at all and wanted to see me fail. My Mom passing at the age of 48. My dad's illnesses. The many rejections I received from high schools, colleges and pro teams. Any of life's happenings that occur be it my fault or not, any of the "dirt" could have buried me but I didn't let it. I would not let it. My teams. They could have been buried as well but they were tough young men who had goals and made damn sure they were going to achieve those goals...be it on the field or off. Again, "We were planted, not buried"

YOUR NOTES

Chapter 36

GREAT LEADERS, GREAT PEOPLE

Now let me talk to you about some of the great Coaches I worked for. My high school coach at Quaker Valley was Rich Woznicki. I cannot tell you how much fun I had playing under Coach Woz. He allowed his players to enjoy the game. But he and I were more than just player and coach. We became friends. I could talk to coach about anything. I would visit him in his office after lunch every day. Having said that, we didn't hit it off right away. When I made varsity my junior year one of coaches' rules were no white baseball shoes. Well I always wore white shoes because one of favorite athletes wore them. Joe Namath. So my first day of practice, Coach Woz comes over to me puts his big hand on my shoulder and in his deepest voice says "Claud, no white shoes!" I said "Coach, my parents bought me these nice white Puma baseball shoes and paid $25.00 for them (This was in 1980) I would hate to just get rid of them." He said, "Then dye them black" There was no way I was doing that. I figured once he seen me play well, he would let it go...he did. He would give me "That look" but I was able to wear the white shoes. But then I pushed him a little further. I was playing right field and a fly ball comes to me. I made something called a "Basket Catch" For those who don't know, it's where the palm of your glove is facing up and you catch the ball below your waist. It's kind of a flashy way to catch a ball. It was made famous by Roberto Clemente, Willie Mays and my favorite, Lee Mazzilli. I wasn't trying to be disrespectful that's just the way I played. So as I come in, he said "Claud, nice catch! Now sit down you are done!" He benched me! He later got kicked out of the game and I was glad! But he knew I was not being disrespectful, and we became best of friends. So much so that he hired me to be his assistant coach after I graduated high school. Coach was tough and you did not want to mess with him, but he was always great with the players. Again, we were close. Even after he retired and I was coaching college ball he would come to my games. I Miss Coach. He gave me my first job and I will forever be appreciative.

Another coach I worked with was Larry Palochek. Everyone knows him as Tank. Tank hired me to be his assistant coach at the Community College of Beaver County. He trusted me and gave me a lot of responsibilities. He was a very secure coach and person. Was always kind to me. When he left coaching, let's just say he was a huge reason why it was me who replaced him. I still contact Tank to this day out of the blue, to thank him for what he did for me. Again, when I think of Tank, I think of Knowledgeable baseball coach, great with players, great with everyone. Very secure as a leader...trusting. And again, great person.

Coach Ed Driscioll. Big, big man. Intimidating. It would be freezing outside and he would wear shorts. But really a soft, gentle man who cared for his players and his programs at Quigley Catholic High School. He too trusted me and I will forever be grateful that I had the chance to work with him.

These three men were not only good coaches who knew the game, but they were great people. I looked forward to seeing them every day. I learned from them. After all these years I still think of them, thank them and have a special place in my heart for them. Wouldn't you rather have your employees; your players say nice things about you than bad? Now you might be saying something like, "As long as we win", or "As long as we all made money, they will have good thoughts of me". No, I don't think so. They will have memories of winning and or making money but you as a person? Let's make sure it's a good situation for everyone involved.

Some other leaders I studied who had impact on me--

- » Jimmy Burchfield Sr.
- » Sam LoFaso
- » John Gaetano
- » Jimmy Amato
- » Lee Davis
- » Chuck Knox

Chapter 37

GREAT QUESTIONS

Here are some great questions I have been asked over the years and my answers.

*What if I am good with my group
but they do not respond in kind?*

Not everyone is going to let their guard down and show you how they feel. That's just how some people are wired. Maybe in time they will come around...maybe not. If they do not, I would say talk with them, ask if there is a problem. They may very well say no problem but they just do not display their emotions much or they are more reserved. That's okay. As long as they are doing their job and being respectful, then you let people be who they are. But again, they must do their job, be respectful and do not stop or impede others from being who THEY are.

*I am not one to show emotion.
I do my job the best I can but am not a real talkative person.
Will this make me less effective as a Leader?*

No. Again, if you try to be something or someone you are not, it will not work. The one coach I mentioned earlier, one time prior to a road trip started to ask me questions about my girlfriend and my Dad. I thought to myself, "He rarely even talks to me, doesn't really like me and all of a sudden he is asking me these questions?" I knew it was from the "Neck up" Not the "Heart up" I say to you, as long as you are doing your job, helping others do theirs well, and are contributing to a good culture for everyone to work in, then again, be yourself.

What if I want to be more expressive? I want to get closer to my team, but every time I do I say the wrong thing or just act dumb. I feel so uncomfortable. What then?

If you really want to have a better relationship with your team, simply tell them. Get out of your comfort zone and communicate. I have a friend who was not very talkative person at all, but he wanted to do some acting. Crazy thing is when the lights were turned on, he was fantastic! He could really talk! As soon as the lights went off, he shut it off as well. Is this bad? No, not at all. He just turned it on when he had to. You can do that. Also, another thing that may help is to tell your team ahead of time, "Look I am not very comfortable talking in front of groups. It doesn't mean that I don't care. I will work on it, just try to understand where I am coming from" In other words, again, communicate. This way your team will not have to guess if you like them or are there for them. Now you may be asking me, "What about that coach you were talking about that tried to talk to you and you said it was fake? Not sincere? Well that guy had a history of being an idiot.

After he asked me those questions, I of course answered them and that was the last time he ever asked me anything personal again. He was doing it "From the neck up"

What if our team is not winning? Or not very successful. It's hard to be kind, or happy and positive.

It is but that is when you have to "Turn it up" even more! Obviously find out why things are not going well. Is it a lack of talent? Lack of a good attitude? What? Figure it out and work on it! You have been positive? Be more positive. You have been communicating with your team? Communicate even more! Turn it up! If it is lack of talent, if you can get better talent, then do it. If you cannot and have to work with what you have, then work even harder! Communicate even more! Try to put them in a position where they have a better chance to succeed. Example for that would be if I have a guy who is 6'4 230 pounds who can hit the ball a mile, I will not ask him to be a stolen base threat. I do not want to put him in a spot where he will fail. He will be my #4, clean-up hitter. That's where the power guys bat. Now I am giving him a chance to succeed with the talent he has to offer us. And vice versa with a guy who is 5'11 195 who can fly on the bases. I will not ask him to be my home run guy. He will be a stolen base threat, disruptor on the bases, etc. Put people in a position to succeed. Then when you are touching success, it will be easier to be kind, happy, emotional. The pillows are softer, the water is colder, winning/success does that.

> *I have a group that is very quiet, yet professional. They do their job, they do it well but I am a talker! I am emotional. I don't know if my attitude will resonate with them. What should I do?*

Great question. I really believe if people are working hard, successful, then you let the plane keep flying! You may have to make the adjustment. Still do your thing yes, but maybe tone it down a bit. I am confident that if things are good in the productivity area, and you show appreciation your workers will "loosen up a little". I would say they will come closer to being like you than you becoming closer to how they are. But at the end of the day, the quote from former Middleweight Boxing Champion & Hall of Farmer Rocky Graziano once said, "Let people be who they are"

> *I was an Assistant to the Leader of the group. Now I am the Leader of the group. I had a great relationship with the team but now as a Leader do I behave the same way? Do I still maintain those close relationships, or do I change?*

I have been in that same spot…a few times. Look, there is no question that the Leader, Head Coach is the guy who not only has the final word but also determines who stays and who doesn't (in a way) I was an assistant Baseball Coach at the age of 18. I was coaching a few of my best friends and a few guys who I had gone to school with or was teammates with for years. I put it on them. I said yes, I am the assistant coach I will treat you the way I always have. But at the same time YOU (The player or employee) cannot say, "Hey this is Claudio. He is our friend. We can do what we want. We can slide a little." Don't do that to me. Do not put me in a bad spot. We can still be friends but just show me the respect I have earned as a friend and the respect I have earned as a coach. As a Head Coach, I had to do and say the same thing. At the end of the day, if your team changes, and tries to take advantage of your friendship, your age then you know what, they are not the person you want on your team. Maybe, just maybe you can continue to be friends, it will be tough but maybe you can do it, but as a team member, it's not going to work. At the same time, I know a guy who was the Assistant GM for years for this one company. He was good to the employees, always had an ear to lend them. They loved him. BUT as soon as he took over as the GM, he changed. Door was closed. Attitude was much different. He made sure to tell the he was in charge all the time. They knew he was in charge and were happy for him. None of them changed the way they were with him or their work efforts. He just developed an elitist type attitude. Became very arrogant. It seemed like he wasn't there to help then anymore. Wasn't there to create a good, positive culture anymore. He was there to show who the boss was and the power he had. Well, needless to say, it all lasted less than 3 years. He was asked to retire and everyone was glad he was gone.

The day I received this question I heard an interview with a well-known NHL Coach. When he was an Assistant coach, he became good friends with this one particular player. The Assistant coach became the Head Coach of another team. They signed the player as a free agent. The Coach was asked how the relationship has changed if at all. "We are still friends, but he knows that I am the Head Coach now and I get paid to win. If he is a part of the lineup that I feel will help us win, great, if not he will just have to understand and adapt to the role he is being asked to fill. We have spoken about it. We are both professionals. We will deal with it professionally." Both had a talk about it. Both were very mature and professional about it. This is the best way to handle it. Communicate.

I was asked to be the President of a Company. They have been successful doing what they have been doing. They really liked the former President of the company. Do I implement my philosophies OR just keep doing what has been working?

Of course, I could just use the old saying" If it ain't broke, don't fix it" But at the same time, would you be true to yourself? I say this, look at the entire package of the team. Okay, they are doing well. The culture is good, but I am sure there is SOMETHING that can be improved! Not even CHANGED but IMPROVED. Don't just change for the sake of changing, no. But do your due diligence, talk with your people and see what can be done better, more often, or maybe even done less. In other words, COMMINICATE! As far as replacing the popular, successful Leader, I am not saying to say this but it just comes to mind. Walter Alston was the manager for the Brooklyn/L.A. Dodgers for 22 years. Under his helm the Dodgers won 4 World Series Championships, won 2,040 games. Alston was voted into the Baseball Hall of Fame. When he retired, the Dodgers named Tommy Lasorda as the new manager. Lasorda was asked "Don't you feel pressure on you? He answered, "Want to know something? I am worried about the guy who's going to replace me!" Lasorda went on to win 2 World Series

Championships with the Dodgers and being inducted into the Baseball Hall of Fame. Alston's nickname was "The Quiet man" meanwhile Lasorda was known for his quick wit, his insightful and funny quotes and big personality. They were both successful and they did it their own way. But on top of that, you had a guy coming into a successful situation and he had the confidence to not only carry on the great Dodger tradition but enhance it.

How about if I have a way for doing something that I know is right, but others do it a different way what should I do? Conform? In other words, should I be a lone wolf?

Here is something that I as a Coach have had to deal with.

I am really good when it comes to teaching hitting. At the risk of sounding arrogant, I will put my knowledge about hitting and how to teach it and make my hitters better up against ANYONE! Having said that, I truly feel hitting is the worst taught thing in sports. I am not going to do a hitting lesson here (That's for another book!) If a player comes to me either for a private hitting lesson or one of the players I coach on my team, and he does "everything wrong" but still hits, I leave him alone! Keep hitting like that! BUT, if he is not hitting, then it's my job to help him get better. Now, the things that most coaches teach when it comes to hitting are so, so wrong! I can prove it too. Anyway, the things I teach are pretty much opposite of what's being taught. Again, I prove to each of my players why the things they were taught do not work on a higher level. So I get the question, "You say not to do it Coach, but just about every coach I have had, plus a lot of Major League Players and announcers say to do it like that. Why are they wrong and you are right? Who should I listen too?"

Great question, and a tough question. This does not just have to be about Hitting a baseball. It could be about investing, building, cooking, how to run a particular business, insert your business instead of hitting. Here are my thoughts on this.

1. An old shampoo commercial of the 70's when like this: "I told someone about this shampoo, and they told someone, and so on, and so on and so on…in other words, things get carried on. Right or wrong. So a bunch of people are teaching this particular-way. They figure if this guy says it, and he is at the top of this sport or business it must be right! Two things about these last two statements:

A. "If 50,000 people say a stupid thing…it is still a stupid thing!"

B. "What do you call a guy who finished last in Med school? A Doctor"

In other words, you who is reading this right now, let's say your name is James. If 50,000 people say your name is Tom, is it Tom? No! It's still wrong!

And think about this for a second. Look at your line of work, whatever it is. Is everyone who is The President, Head Coach, GM, CEO good at what they do? I bet not. So in other words, just because a person is high up the ladder, or everyone is saying/teaching the same thing, that does not mean it is the RIGHT THING!

Do your due diligence. See if they are indeed correct. If not see what IS correct and teach it! Do not worry about the masses. If you feel that you studied something a great deal, know how to articulate it, PROVE you are right, then DO IT!

Should I be a hands-on type and run everything or let my people do their own thing with little input from me?

My favorite golfer and favorite businessman Greg Norman was asked how he runs his business employees. His answer was "Loose, Tight". You want them to do their thing. Add to the potential success of the team. You want them to feel they have their signature on the team and its success. You want them to lead as well. But at the same time, you have to inject what you feel is best for your team and for the team's individuals. Make them better. Give them more confidence. This way, when it is time for them to lead or make a choice, YOU are confident in it because you taught them, or enhanced their knowledge. Example, I let my catchers call pitches. Why? I let them know things to look for on the opposing batter. What holes he has in his swing. Talk to him about what to look for in our pitcher as well as what to usually throw on certain counts and of course keeping the hitter off balance. So if they learn and know all of that, I trust them to call the game! Simple! Same with defensive calls on certain game situations. I let my SS or 3B (depending on who is the veteran) call the defensive positioning with runners on 1st & 3rd. Now having said all of that, if there is a pattern of pitches or a defensive play call that I do not agree with, I will change it or discuss it with them. But that rarely happens. Now when it comes to offense, I do 100% of the play calling, including giving them the "Green Light" (which mean either steal if you want or swing at the next pitch if you want) When observing my hitters during the game, I am always reminding them if they are making a mistake. In other words, all hitters have a "Glitch". So it's my job to see it and remind them what we worked on to fix it. So back to the Greg Norman quote. "Loose/Tight" I give them room to lead, to do their thing, but I also control certain aspects of the game.

This might be a silly question, but as a Head Coach how do you determine who gets the most playing time?

Excellent question. Simple answer. The players decide who plays the most! Whoever is the better player, whoever is going to contribute to the team winning, on the field and off, plays.

What is the hardest part of your job(s)as a Leader?

As a Head Coach, it's seeing a player who is a good person, working hard not getting the playing time he would like. It's just that the person in front of him is better. Again, I didn't make the decision, the players did. I just saw who the better player was. So you have to sit down with the player who is not getting the playing time he would like and A. Explain why. B. Help that player become better

As a Professional baseball scout, the hardest thing by far is to tell a payer that he is not good enough to play pro baseball. That is deflating to me. You are telling someone that their dreams are not going to come true. BUT I will also tell them something that James L. Gamble (The Owner/Scout of the Pro Scouting Co. I work with, Global Scouting Bureau) always tells players. "Just because I don't think you are good enough to go to the next level does not mean SOMEONE ELSE won't think that you are! I want you to come back to me and say, 'James, you were wrong! I was good enough to play Pro ball'. That would make me happy!" Or I tell them, I did not make Pro baseball as a player. BUT I stuck it out and made it as a Scout and had offers to do it professionally. So there are options.

Speaking of James Gamble, let me say a few things about him. The first thing he said to me was that he wanted to be "Santa Claus" for people. Well he certainly was that for me. He is the most unselfish Leader I have ever known and seen. He does not care to get credit for anything. He truly, truly just wants to help people get to where they want to go. That's it! I have seen him help so many people and not just in baseball but in life! He has actually saved people's lives with things that he has done. And to be honest with you, some of those people have screwed him over. But that's another story. I cannot not say enough great things about James. Again, the reason I am doing what I am doing today and have the life I have today is because of God, My Mom & Dad, my wife Lynda, my daughter Ida, and James Gamble. James is a Leader and lives my Mom's saying of "Lead from the Heart up, Not the Neck up"

> *One of my players just does not talk to me.*
> *Talks and greets everyone but me. (The Head Coach)*
> *Should I do anything about this?*

I had a player do that with me. We had a minor heated discussion during a game and it went south even more after that. I didn't want the relationship to be so cold. So distant...Negative. I would hear him talking about sports and different athletes. So I approached him and another player who were talking about the Pittsburgh Penguins. Then the Pirates. I shared some of my thoughts and stories. This player and I now had a common denominator. Pittsburgh Sports teams! From there I got to know him better, he got to know me better. I would say if our relationship was a 2 out of 10 at one point, it is about a 7.5-8 out of 10 now.

> *What strategies/techniques do you use to keep the team focused on your team goals especially when things are not going well?*

Have a theme for your team to focus on. One particular year we had a very good team. We got off to a bad start. When you have a short season, you cannot afford to get off to a bad start. But we did. So after a loss, I simply told the team, "We have to win 9 out of our next 9 games to have a shot at the playoffs. How do we win 9 in a row? The little boy asked the old man, ' Old man how do you achieve success in life?' The old man answered, ' You achieve success in life by eating an elephant.' The little boy said ' By eating an elephant?? How do you eat an elephant?' The old man said, ' One bite at a time.' Usually when our team broke a huddle we would say, "Win" or our team name " Tartans" but after that talk our team, and chose this on their own, they would break the huddle by saying " Elephants!!!" I knew right then and there we had incredibly special players but more importantly special people. So you are probably asking if we won all 9 games? No. We won 6 in a row, but I cannot tell you how proud I was and am of that special team. So my strategy was simple. Let's win one game at a time. Small bites...small steps. We were focused on the most important game of the year...our next one. Focus. Now having said that, I could have come up with the greatest lines, quotes and heart pounding, passionate emotions in the world BUT if I did not have the "Special" team and people that I had, they would have said, "What do elephants have to do with baseball??" So again, it all goes back to the people you have on your team, staff, organization. If they want it, if they are special, they will get it and your group will have a chance to succeed.

How do you make your team better, more efficient without suppressing them or berating them?

Communicate. Tell the team who you are. On the field and off. Tell them what you expect from them as people and as a team. Be upfront and honest. Tell them that you are here to help make them better as individuals and as a team. You are there to create a positive culture. Hollering or trying to be a "Tough Guy" won't get it done but at the same time, I always ask my teams "Do not turn me into someone I don't want to be. Our relationship will depend on you. If you are great with me, I will be great with you. If you are distant or negative with me, that is the culture that you will live in as long as you are here, which might not be that long. I will say it again, "If we pull the same rope at the same time in the same direction, we will get a great result" Lets pull that rope together so you can be the best version of yourself on the field/office and off.

How do I know if I am working them too hard? Pushing too much?

Great question! In 1993 when I was the Head Coach at Community College of Beaver County, we played doubleheaders every game. I noticed that we would win the first game but the second game we were usually flat. Drained. And sometimes, not all the time but sometimes we would lose but most of the time we did not play as well as we should have. So, I thought the problem was the way I coached. As I mentioned before, I am deeply passionate when I coach, I pace over 4 miles. I drive my teams. I am encouraging them constantly, I coach! I am totally drained after a game. Vince Lombardi once said, "The greatest feeling in the world is to lie exhausted in victory. The second greatest feeling in the world is to lie exhausted in defeat" I always tell my teams that. So, this one particular doubleheader we were playing Carnegie Mellon University! They had not won a game all season. So, I decided that I was going to tone it down. Still coach, still try as hard as possible to win, just not as intense. Not as vocal. 4th inning comes we are down 4-0. CMU is gaining confidence, momentum. I have the guys huddle up prior to our at bat. I asked them, "What is wrong with you guys? You are flat!!" One of my players quietly said, "You don't seem to be in it, so I guess it flowed down to us." Then I "Turned it up" as did the team. We won and won big...Both games. So, what's my point? It is a balancing act. I know that I expect total commitment from my teams and again, I give my all every game. My best advice is to try to pick your spots. As the Kenny Rogers song says "Know when to hold then, know when to fold them. Know when to walk away, know when to run..." Know when to turn it up. Tone it down. You will know. You will get a sense from your team. For me, I am always going to be intense and go at it hard, but I may tone it down a hair here and there to the team. But always be encouraging. Always coach. Always try to win. You will know. I have said in this book to trust your team, well trust yourself as well.

Do You Call Every Pitch, Every Defensive Play, Every Offensive Play For Your Team? In Other Words, Are You 1005 In Control?

I am 100% in control but having said that, I do not call all pitches. We have a game plan as to where to pitch a particular hitter but as far as calling pitches I will add my 2 cents, but I let the pitcher and catcher control that. Why? Let's say I want a curve ball, but the pitcher is not confident in that pitch and or the catcher has seen several of the pitcher's curve ball that day and it's just not there. Why should he throw it? Throw something they are confident in. Again, we have an idea where to throw a pitch, and I will add to the mix, but I have confidence in my pitcher and catcher. We go through things prior to a game. As for defensive play calling. I let my infield captain make that call. They know what pitch is coming, they also know where the hitter's tendencies are because I let them know through my in-game notes I take. Now if they call something I do not like, I will change it. As for offensive play calling, here I would say I control 99.9%.

Coach, I Heard You On An Interview One Time And You Mentioned Real Estate And Leadership. I Missed A Lot Of The Conversation. Do You Remember That Interview And What You Said?

I do remember that comment for sure. I was asked what is the most important thing to build a successful team? To me it is very simple. In real estate the old line is, "The three most important things in real estate are Good location, good location, good location. I say the three most important things to having a good team a good business, really anything are Good people, good people, good people.

I Have Heard You Mention Several Times That Former Nfl Head Coach Chuck Knox Was Like An Uncle To You. Did He Ever Give You Any Coaching Advice?

Chuck Knox meant a ton to me and still does. The two things that stand out in all of our conversations where not just for the coaching notebook, but for life's notebook and they were: " You make your own breaks in life" and " Prepare for everything and be ready for anything".

Coach, I Feel More And More Coaches, And Really Leaders Are Relying Way Too Much On Analytics. What Are Your Thoughts On This?

I agree! Look, numbers are especially important. But you still have to know your business. I sometimes feel people use analytics as a crutch so that if they make a bad move or decision they can always say "Hey, I went by the numbers!" What about if you do not have access to all the numbers/analytics? As I have said many times, I do not have 365 at bats on a hitter or even a scouting report to see what his tendencies are so I better know my business and know it quick. Now if you do have access to all types of info, great! Use it as a reference but in my opinion, I personality would not run my game or business just through those numbers. Again, that's just me.

I Am Working With A Small Company And It Does Not Plan To Go Bigger... I Have Always Wanted To Work With A Bigger Firm. It Is Tough For Me To Stay Focused. Did This Ever Happen To You And If So, How Did You Deal With It?

Great question and I appreciate the honesty. Yes, I was in that position. I was the Junior Varsity coach at a small high school after coaching on the D1 level. I remember coaching our JV team in a tournament and my Dad was in attendance. He said something to me that I will never forget. "You coached that team as if it were the Yankees! You bloomed where you were planted" So I say to you, "Bloom where you are planted. From that small high school I went on to work in professional baseball with the Global Scouting Bureau (I am now with the GSB for 19 years and counting! And am in my 15th year at Carnegie Mellon University as the Head baseball Coach ..and counting) If I would have given the high school team a half halfhearted effort, I do not think I would have done well there or gone on to have the career I am having. And to be honest with you, I absolutely loved coaching there. Yes, I still had my goals and dreams but again, I gave that team everything I had. So give the job you are at now all that you have and then some. Get better at what you do. Bloom where you are planted. From there I think the chances of you climbing the ladder and getting to where you want to go will increase. Plus, the company you are working for thought enough of you to hire you. They gave you a shot. They are paying you. You owe them your best effort.

I Am A First Year Head Coach. My Question To You Is, Do Your Strategies, Emotions, How You Interact With The Team, Ever Change Or Adjusted During A Playoff Or Championship Game?

Love this question! I remember my first playoff game ever. I was walking towards the dugout and I said to myself, " Just because this has the title of ' Playoff game' does not mean that you change the way you coach, handle people or really anything. Do what brought you here." Now having said that, I am always wound up. I always give everything I have for every game. I always push my players and try to wring every bit of energy and success out of my players with every game. So it is expected that we do the same for a playoff game. So to be honest, we are used to feeling that way. As for strategies, again, I do not change one bit. Our teams are aggressive on the base paths, we will do some things that are not " by the book". If I put the brakes on that type of coaching, my players will sense it. Not good. They will think I am coaching scared. Again, to me, just because it has the title " Playoff game" or " Championship game" does not mean you coach any different. Yes, you might be a little more pumped up, excited prior to the game but once the game begins, you just do your job the way you always do it.

*How Are You With Your Team After A Loss?
What Do You Say?*

After every game, win or lose we meet on the foul line. If our dugout is on the third base side, we meet towards left field and first base side right field. If we win, I will go over why we won so we can repeat it... I will talk about some individual plays that happened. Players will get recognized. I always end it with how happy I am for them and how proud I am of them. I will then ask the team leaders and many times any of the players if they have anything to say. If we lose, I make it quick. Basically, what I say is, "We made some mistakes, we will work on them individually at practice and fix things up. See you at practice." Then we simply work on what needs fixed. To holler at them, berate them, blame them does zero! Let's fix things. Make things better. Simple.

*How Do You Handle/Deal With A Player
That Does Not Play Much?*

As I have said before, that is the toughest part of coaching for me. Not being able to play everyone. But on this level, you can't. Now I usually have a 16 to 20-man roster and I would say 11, 12 maybe 13 guys get a bulk of the playing time. I always say it's not up to me who plays, it's up to the players. If you are good, and can help the team win, you play. Simple. But I also try very hard to make sure that the guys who do not play as much get recognized, get the same attention practice wise as the starters. I think it has worked because many of the players who have not played much for us over the years still keep in touch! Now I have been approached by players who were not happy with their playing time or lack thereof. We would talk about. They would give their side, then I would give my side. I do not remember a time where it was loud or ended bad. As a matter of fact, one time, in 1988 my first year as a Head coach, a player came up to me pretty sad. He was going to quit because he was not playing much. But he was sad because he didn't want to upset me. He felt bad that he was quitting. I tried to talk him into staying but I understood where he was coming from. He was a good kid, and I appreciate the respect he showed me. So basically, you treat all of your players like they are important because they are. You treat all of your players like they have a role to the success of the team which they do. Care for your players. Care for your team.

How Do You Improve As A Coach Every Year?

I feel I am a better coach in 2020 than I was in 2019. I will be a better coach in 2021 than I was in 2020. How? I never feel I know enough. I am always watching other coaches and l try to earn what they do right, see what they do wrong. I have a notebook that I still have that I keep in front of me while I watch games on TV and I keep it with me in my brief case. I listen to interviews and read a ton. Not just in baseball either. All sports. As far as the technical side of things I am lucky to know a lot of former major league baseball players and I ask them many questions. Quick example, 1979 World Series Champion for the Pittsburgh Pirates Grant Jackson who pitched in the majors for 18 years and coached for a number of years said something to me so simple, so common sense but I never heard it before so I never looked for it before. He said, "When a pitcher is leaning towards the catcher and is off balance, he is throwing because he has to. If he is balanced, he is throwing because he wants to." He said this to me about 10 years ago. I was 46. So my point is I am always on the lookout to improve. Never feel that you know it all. When you do, you get lazy. When you get lazy, you will not be coaching long. Always study. One time it was 2am in the morning and I could not sleep. I turned on the TV and there was a celebrity softball game on. There was not an athlete on the field. They all had bad swings, BUT when they did the things that I teach (I will spare you the hitting lesson) they hit the ball! So all that did was reinforce what I teach is correct. Again, my point is I am always on the lookout to get better.

I Have Heard You Say How Confident You Are As A Coach, But Never Be Arrogant. Could You Explain That Further?

Thank you for that question. I am extremely confident in what I can do as a coach. I am extremely confident I can help make a player better, a team better, but at the same time if I act like an idiot, or be arrogant, who cares how good I am because my bad attitude will overshadow how good I am. Not only that, but I also know this: "It's a quick trip from the penthouse to the outhouse". Don't get too full of yourself. Again, be confident in what you do and how you do it but you do not have to be arrogant about it. I remember one time I was at a hitting facility and this guy was just walking around the place big timing everyone. I mean he wasn't walking; he was striding! So I asked a person who worked there, "Who is that guy?" He said, "Oh, he is the 8U coach who won the tournament last week." I said to myself, I know Boxing Champions, World Series Champions, Super Bowl Champions and THEY don't act like this guy does! Confident, yes. Arrogant, no!

I have to add this story. My dad, Olindo had real bad circulatory issues with his right leg. We went to 5 Doctors, if I am not mistaken all 5 said they would have to amputate. They were all sure of it. Knee down, amputate. Obviously, we were devastated. Well a friend of mine had a wife that was a nurse, so she recommended a Doctor by the name of Paul Collier. Well we figured why not! What is the worst thing that he could say? Amputate? So we went in, my Dad took a bunch of x rays, tests for Dr. Collier to look at. So he walks in and says this: "Well, you have had several surgeries on that leg so there isn't a whole lot for me to work with, BUT I can save your leg." So my Dad said, "But 5 other Doctors all said that they would have to amputate for sure!" It was almost like my Dad was trying to talk Dr. Collier out of the positive message he just gave us! Then Dr. Collier very confidently said and just a side note, he had no idea I worked in baseball, " If the bases are loaded I want to be the pitcher on the mound with the ball in my hand to end the game!" As soon as he said that, me and my Dad knew we hit it right with this guy. Well, he was able to save my Dad's legs, and not only that but my Dad and I consider Dr. Collier and his wife Nancy friends. My Dad passed in 2004 and Dr. Collier was one of the Pal bearers. But his confidence just hit us. Gave us hope. I will never forget his words but also how he said it. Very matter of fact.

I will add one more story. Carnegie Mellon baseball had not had a winning season in a long, long, long time. As a matter of fact, from what I heard, they had not won a game in a few years. So, during the interview I was asked how long it would take for me to turn things around. I said, "As soon as I sign the contract and walk in the door." Cocky? Arrogant? No not at all. Confident. Self-assured? Yes. How about if I would have said, " Oh I am not sure" or " I will do my best and we will see what happens" Or if Dr. Collier would have said, " I will try my best and we will go from there." So our first year we had 10 wins, 11 losses. And we just kept building the program from there. I have had special people and special players...that helps...a ton!

What Are Your Thoughts On Having Team Leaders? How Much Responsibility Do I Give Them?

I think it is a must. It is always good to have strong team leaders. It is always good for your players or employees to hear another voice… But giving the same message. Plus, it forms a very strong team bond. As far as how much responsibility to give them? I think things have a way of morphing into whatever they become. Again, as long as they serve and put out the same message that you are, having team leaders is very important.

Say You Have A Star Player Or A Star Employee, A Key Component To Your Teams Success But Is A Real Problem In The Dugout Or In The Office. They Have A Real Attitude And Act Like A Prima Dona, They Put Their Individual Success in Front Of The Teams Success.
How Do You Deal With A Person Like That?

Again, first you try like crazy to communicate with this person. Show them the error of their ways. To put their feet in the teams or other employees' shoes to see how that person would feel. Try to show them what I say all the time, " If we all pull the same rope at the same time in the same direction for the same purpose, we will get a special result" If this does not work, then that person has to go. Try everything you can do to help this person be a better team player, but if it does not get the result you want, again, time to move on. Remember these two lines, "You didn't get rid of this person, they got rid of themselves." And, "An aching tooth is better out than in."

What Rules Do You Have For Your Team?

Rule 1. Care. Care for the entire team.

Rule 2. Never disrespect me.

Rule 3. Give me everything you have.

Then we talk about those three sets of rules as umbrellas. Under each are a list of common-sense things like caring for the team/players on the field and off. Don't disrespect me, the school, your teammates, yourself etc.

I Like To Delegate As A Leader. Your Thoughts On That Style?

If that is your style and you not only have a great staff of people that you trust to delegate to but it's also successful, then keep at it. At the same time, when this question comes up, I think of former NFL Head Coach and family friend Chuck Knox's line on this: "I have seen where the offensive coordinator is in charge of the offense. The defensive coordinator is in charge of the defense, the special team's coach is in charge of the special teams and then you have the Head coach who is in charge of nothing!" Yes, give your assistants a job and freedom to do it. But for me, I like to be very hands on. Not in a "Boss way" but just getting things done right. Again, I will let my assistant do their thing, but I will oversee it and tweak if I have to. I will never be totally out of the picture.

Your Thoughts On Team Meetings?

I rarely have team meetings. Yes, have them when needed but if you have too many, it loses its impact. Most of the time if something needs said I go to the individual. If a team meeting is needed cut to the chase. Say what you have to say, get a response and move forward. No need for a long, long meeting. Again, it will lose its impact. I remember one time we had a few things happen to our team. I called a team meeting. I think the guys thought I was going to have a ton to say, and it would be a long meeting. I got in front of the team, and simply said "It happened. We will deal with it. And we will move forward." One of our players even had T-Shirts made with that on it. It was effective.

Coach I Have Tried To Reward My Players For Good Effort, Big Wins Etc... I Might Give Them A Day Off, Or Game Balls That Type Of Thing. I Was Told By An Older Coach Not To Do That. Your Thoughts?

I think it's great! I look at it as not a reward, but an appreciation of what they have done for the team and for me. A "Thank you" of sorts. Let me also add this. We have started a Carnegie Mellon University baseball Hall of Fame. We have an awards banquet. Those are always tough. Emotional. I have named 5 awards after 4 players who played for me (1 I was asked to name after a young man I was not fortunate enough to coach, Daniel Purpera. (Defensive player of the year) He passed away in a car accident and his teammates thought enough of him to want him honored and I am honored to do it.) We have the "Jon Coens Pitcher of the year". "James Langhauser Offensive player of the year". "Brian Tabata Toughest Player of the year" and the "Wade Brogdon Leadership Award" Those four players turned our program not only into a winning program but an important program. I wanted to show them how much I appreciated what they did for the team and for me.

I also started an Unofficial program where I help guys get internships and jobs. We have helped guys (and in one case their future wife) get jobs in the medical field, architecture world, finance, and sports. Again, I am their coach and want to help not just on the field but off the field. And since I do some TV shows and a podcast, we have some fun with that and have them on as guests. I call all of these things,

"Another flower in the garden." Again, I want to make it a great experience for them, on the field and off.

Chapter 38

TWO GREAT LEADERS, MY MOM AND DAD

My Leaders...Olindo & Ida Reilsono.
(Photo courtesy of the author)

I mention my Mom (Ida) and Dad (Olindo) all the time. Because they deserve it. You want to talk about Leadership? My Mom & Dad were great Leaders. Quickly, my Dad went through hell in his life. His Mom passing away at the age of 52, first wife passed at the age of 32 leaving behind 2 young kids. In 1969, (I was 4) He was told he was going to go blind and that he had emphysema. Saving all of the story for another book, but he had a lot on his plate. He basically had a nervous breakdown where he got to the point that he could not leave past our hedges. He developed a phobia. Well for two and a half years my Dad could not work. He owned a lawn maintenance business and worked in the Steel Mill. But for those two and a half years we had no money coming in. We had 7 people in our house. None of us missed a beat. I always said my Dad knew how to make a buck and my Mom knew how to save and spread it. In 1971 my Dad decided to start the Lawn maintenance business back up by hiring a couple of people to work it. Then in 1972, he started to be able to go out slowly but surely to work himself as long as I or my Mom was able to go with him. Then as the years went by he was able to go and do things himself. He overcame the phobia. Now what about him going blind and having emphysema you may ask? Just telling you the truth here, Whenever I would pass our Church, I would always pray "Please don't let my Daddy go blind" Didn't know what emphysema was. But anyway, my Dad never went blind. As a matter of fact, he was an excellent target shooter! And he never had emphysema. Say what you want. Think whatever it is you want to think. If my Dad was here now, he would tell you it was due to my prayers...and I believe it! So, one time I asked him, "Dad, you went through so much. You had so many health issues, so many people let you down, tragedies in your life, how did you come back and overcome all of them? "he simply said, "I had to. I had you to raise. I wanted to do all I could for you" That's Leadership. My Mom kept the ship afloat and it was not easy. Not only did she have to manage the money, but take care of my Dad during his illness, take care of her baby (Me) and raise 2 of my Dad's other kids (which was a task to say the least- Again, next book) and help raise my half-sisters baby. Again, not easy. But she did it. No excuses. No hollering. No placing blame. No passing on responsibilities to anyone. She just did it. Simple. That's Leadership. Let's jump ahead. On October 8, 1988 my wonderful Mom passed at the age of 48. On February 19, 2004, my wonderful Dad passed at the age of 75. They gave me the opportunity to make all of my dreams come true. Without them, trust me, trust me, I would NOT have the life I have today. I can go and on about them, but I will stick to the Leadership part. They went through so much but they Lead. They didn't complain. They saw what the situation was, came up with a game plan, accepted the fact that it was going to be tough and did it. Before every game I had as a player of Coach as I left the door, my Mom would always give me a hug, and kiss and say in Italian "Mostrare lono il tuo coraggio!" Translated, "Show them your Courage" That's what they did. They showed their courage. They did what they had to do. They made tough decisions. Growing up, I had some "family members" really on me about my dream of being in professional baseball. They would say the meanest things. "Time to grow up, quit baseball and be a man" "You will never make it." " it's a pipe dream" " Quit buffaloing everyone including yourself, you won't make it" " Be realistic" I have to add this, When my Mom passed, the first day of her viewing, as I walked towards the casket for the first time, this one " family member" who let's just say used to fluff his hair on top to cover the horns, said to me " Now it's really time to quit baseball and be a man" Rotten person. But this is how it went for years and years. I mean they were so passionate about me quitting. Not because they cared, or they were worried about me not having a backup plan. No. They were just jealous and sick people. Bad people. They had good careers they just didn't want me to have my dreams come true. Again, bad people. Anyway, when my parents would hear these lovely quotes, man did they get fired up! Both of them would snap out on those idiots! And I mean snap out! Again, being my parents, Leaders, they defended what they believed in, that was me.

Which leads to my next point about Leadership. Believe in your group, team. Believe in the individuals. One of my favorite people ever and a friend, former NCAA Champion Basketball Coach, Jim Valvano once said "My Dad (Rocco Valvano) gave me the biggest present anyone can give another. He believed in me" I have a plaque at my parents' grave site that says the same thing. If you show belief in your team, show them kindness, understanding, loyalty, love, passion, communicate, honesty, intelligence, heart, courage, confidence, be approachable, your team will not want to disappoint you. They will go through a wall for you. When they speak of you, they will speak in glowing terms. When they come across an obstacle in life, they will be reminded of you, your quotes, your actions. You will have had impact on their careers and lives. Again, Jim Valvano once said that his favorite word in the dictionary was the word "Impact" So have Impact.

There you have it. Short and sweet. Keep this with you. Read it. Re read it. Do you have to do everything the exact same way? Of course not. All I can say to you is this is the way I did it. The way I am doing it. I truly hope this helps you in your work as a Leader. Wishing you all the best…and remember "Lead from the Heart up, Not the Neck up"

TESTIMONIALS

Here are just some of the special people I have had the honor and privilege to coach over the years. They are as far back as my first year as a Head Coach, 1988 and as recent as 2020. I appreciate all of their kind words. Its people like this that make it special.

******

COLLIN SAMPLE

My name is Collin Sample and I am currently at football coach and Earth/Space Science teacher Seminole high school in Sanford, FL. I have been teaching now 24 years and a football coach for 26 years. I played football, baseball and basketball at Quaker Valley High School in Leetsdale, PA. More importantly, I feel extremely BLESSED for the positive experiences and life-long lessons learned in these athletic programs during those short 3 years of time. I was a 3.3 GPA from a lower middle-income but hard-working family, trying to fit in the upper middle-class world our school was somewhat like. I just wanted to share some of the positive impacts that the Quaker Valley HS athletics program, especially the Quakers' baseball program (lead by Coach Claudio Reilsono), had upon my life and the success I have had the last quarter century!

Coming into Quaker Valley HS, I was well-liked but still did not have much self-confidence and found myself looking up to others at school. Instead, I was that person who was entrenched in a mindset where I did not take the initiative to lead or compete due to the tentativeness, I had about being the focus of attention. However, as I became part of the Quaker baseball program and began to have interaction with Coach Reilsono, I was able to gain confidence as an athlete that I did not have before. This process took the whole 3 years and was slow, but it enabled me to rise from the depths of self-doubt.

The attribute that still sticks with me as a coach now, that I inherited subliminally from Coach Reilsono, is RELATABILITY. The first thing you must do to be a great coach is to make connections with your players. That was the first thing he did as the assistant varsity coach my sophomore & junior years. Coach did that with his infectious personality, comical wit and focus as a listener when hearing out players concerns or hardships. This immediately let a player know that he was INVESTED IN YOU. As an athlete that is when you realize, look if they are willing to do that as an adult, and I am not their kid, I better return that favor in effort to this person because they have my back. He MAINTAINED these relationships after the season was over as well...going to our basketball or football games and even making some of us football players numbered towels for us to sport during our games.

This connectivity enabled him to be a prime example of HOW TO ENJOY not only what you do but the people you are doing it with. This focus of making the daily routine enjoyable enabled us to put in the hard work to be successful and not view it like was detrimental...just positive necessity. This enables coaches to push athletes further so they can accomplish greater feats together. This continued to build the TRUST in a coach, who was young at the time, but KNOWLEDGEABLE with what he would explain to us with his HANDS-ON INSTRUCTION. This enabled us to see immediate results and the combination of those 3 aspects made his constructive criticism for success more audible to his players.

The investment in us enabled us play hard for him, which in turn enabled him to gain trust in us. That is when he ENTRUSTED PLAYERS WITH RESPONSIBILITY.This especially led to a point of my maturation during our Senior year. He made me Co-Captain of the team with Jason Terosky...a guy who I looked to as a leader. Not only did he say you guys are on the same level, he trusted me to call all the pitches during the games for Jason! What a CONFIDENCE BOOSTER. This made me more assertive in other aspects of my game and life in general. I really gave me the confidence to COMPETE WITHOUT THE WORRY OF FAILURE.

The mindset of confidence was also instilled in us through the HIGH PROGRAM EXPECTATIONS and holding us ACCOUNTABLE to those goals & guidelines. The mindset of making our school proud but more importantly, not letting down the LEGACY of our successful baseball program was of utmost importance...we are SUPPOSED TO WIN! This entailed the necessary positive and negative motivation tactics of successful programs. If Coach Reilsono or Coach Woznicki felt a butt chewing or running consequence was needed to refocus a winning mentality, then it would be exacted. TEAM SUCCESS was the only thing tolerable.

However, Coach Reilsono showed us that the individuals involved in the winning program were important also. We, as individual players, had our own dreams and aspirations for greatness as well. We would see the great athletes before us in the NFL or Major League baseball on TV and around us at the grocery store. Coach's family was a good example of how we could be one of them, even coming from the small town of Sewickley, PA. We knew coach's father, but then found out he was close friends with Coach Chuck Knox, a head coach in the NFL. But to our surprise, we found out that he was a graduate of Quaker Valley HS!!!! This just told us that we can be something big as well. So dream on, work hard and be passionate...it can happen.

Coach Reilsono also showed us to be PASSIONATE in what you love. Whether it was BEING AUTHORITATIVE to get our focus, being ENTHUSIASTIC during practice, PRAISING successes or TEACHING THE FUNDAMENTALS of the game or life, we always could sense that passion for what he did and for his family as well. The passion was demonstrated in many forms. I have seen it celebrating championships, breaking a pitch counter/being ejected while standing up to an umpire for a called 3rd strike or crying with players at the disappointment of losing a playoff game. All things that I do know with my players.

These combinations of characteristics demonstrated to us daily HOW TO BE A MAN OF

"MANY HATS". We learned how to be serious and focused one moment, then be able to have a laugh with others at a different moment...how lead when called on and when to fall in line when needed. It has shaped all of us to be successful people, great fathers, respectful sons/brothers, helpful neighbors, positive community members and PROUD QUAKERS WHO DO WHAT IS RIGHT AND STRIVE FOR GREATNESS!

Thanks Coach Reilsono & GO QUAKERS!

******

JOHN COENS
(CARNEGIE MELLON- 2010)

Claudio was the first coach of mine to approach the game as a mentor and friend rather than a drill Sargent. I watched him time and again get to know someone and meet them where they are to get the most out of them in baseball. This led to a cohesive community of players working under Claudio's guidance to win, but also ensure we were all enjoying the game

******

WADE BROGDON
(CARNEGIE MELLON- 2012)

Coach Claudio is a Coach, and person, like no other. During my 3-year career at Carnegie Mellon University, from 2010-2012, I had the distinct pleasure of playing for Claudio. Immediately, I knew we would go on to do great things together. His coaching style is built around getting the most out of every player. All while maintaining a high overall standard, he expected even more from better players, never letting starters be satisfied.

From a technical baseball standpoint, the best thing Claudio reinforced and taught me, was to treat hitting a baseball like you're a boxer preparing for a fight. He would have me take my batting stance, then replace the bat with my fist, and have me punch a bag. The position from which I could deliver the most power and biggest pop, was now my 'load position'. I had never been exposed to something that simple yet so productive. I went on to bat over .400 in my career, and much of it had to do with my shift in stance and approach.

One of my fondest memories of playing for Coach was from my first games with the team. We were playing in the 2010 spring break tournament in Tampa, Florida. My grandparents, who I was incredibly fond of, were experiencing declines in health at the time. They had loved seeing me play high school ball, and I didn't think at the time that they'd be able to come and see me play again. Well, my mother surprised me by bringing them both down to Tampa to watch the few game stretch. During my third at bat, I told my grandpa I was going to 'Hit a Bomb' for him, and then subsequently took a fastball deep to left center. Coach knew how important it was for me to have that moment with my grandpa and made sure someone from the bench went to find the exact ball and bring it back so that I could give it to my grandpa. That was the last time my grandparents saw me play, and it's a moment I'll always cherish. That's just the type of guy Coach Claudio is, always looking to be helpful, and looking for a deeper personal meaning beyond sports.

To this day, nearly 8 years after my last game at Carnegie Mellon, we continue to have a close relationship. He is constantly checking in on myself and my family and continues to involve those who played for him in his life. Claudio simply 'gets it' as a coach and a man. One of the key components to leadership is having the continued respect of people you work/play with. Claudio not only commands respect, but he continues to earn it.

******

TIM LIU (CARNEGIE MELLON-2020)

Playing for Coach Claudio has been one of the best experiences I've had as a ballplayer. Not only does Coach understand how to teach the fundamentals, but he's got an incredibly astute eye for the game at all levels. I always come away from baseball talks with Coach with a new found appreciation for the subtleties of the game; from breaking down last night's Pirates game to analyzing a batter's hands when he swings, I feel that I am always learning from Coach.

One thing I appreciate about Coach is his ability to adapt his coaching style to players with all sorts of skill sets. He doesn't force players to go outside of their comfort zone, and instead, he focuses on identifying and building their strengths. For instance, I may not be the hardest thrower on the mound, but Coach doesn't go out of his way to try and make me add velocity; instead, he focuses on my off-speed pitches and helps me strategize ways to creatively attack each batter. Coach understands how to recognize skill sets and bring out the best in each player.

But most importantly, I am grateful for the personal relationship I've built with Coach. Whether it's receiving a text from him during the summer asking how my family and I are doing, or him asking me about the new restaurant my girlfriend and I tried recently, Coach genuinely cares about each and every one of his players as though they are part of his own family. He was one of the first people I communicated with during the recent COVID-19 pandemic, and that speaks volumes to the impact he's had on me as an individual. It's these little things that make me see Coach Claudio as not just a mentor, but as a friend. He's the type of coach I want to play for.

******

DOM PERRY
(DUQUESNE UNIVERSITY-1996)

I grew up in a small, blue-collar, steel town. People are tough there and the economy was in rough shape when I was a kid in the late 70s and 80s so feelings and the discussion thereof were not really on anyone's respective radars. If people cared, they didn't talk about it much! Coaches were tough, yelled A LOT and thought the best way to get the most out of you was to mentally and physically punish you to both make you hard and mean and also as a way to weed out the weak. Your parents were not going to call a coach-no way. Coach said it - you did it - no discussion, no input. You just played to win! Winning was the only time you were certain everyone would be happy albeit briefly until the world's realities reappeared. And… well… that was the routine; just the way it was.

I arrived at Duquesne University as a young, impressionable 17-year-old expecting much of the same. I chose Duquesne because it was away from home but not too far; similar city type so I expected the values and people to be the same or similar. I was excited to play Division 1 baseball in a good conference in a competitive environment. This was a young team. Lots of incoming freshman and some talented sophomores. Not many upper classmen due to a recent coaching change. I expected to win but maybe not right away. I was realistic in that we needed a year or more to be competitive and were maybe going to take some lumps and probably get yelled at a bunch! What I did not expect was how our coaches would approach the game -as individuals whose collective efforts were needed for the team to win. A VERY different leadership style for me!!

Our coaches had a very different approach to the game of baseball which was well beyond what I expected and very much a welcome change. For the first time in life, I experienced what I now would call players' coaches. They cared. I spent the most time with our hitting coach, Claudio Reilsono. First, I never called a teacher, coach or any adult for that matter by their first name for fear my mother would find out and smack me! So when I met coach and he said, "call me Claudio" I was taken back. He asked me questions about me and what made me "tick" as he would say. Then came the encouragement to make my own goals that coach would review, refine and build a plan around. Then the extra time devoted, well, well beyond "office hours" of coach talking me through some different ways to accomplish said goals that I had not considered. A thinking person's approach; a mental game; a strategy behind the work; technical knowledge; adjustments; film study-these were all new concepts to me that allowed me to improve immensely in college. We laughed at mistakes and moved on, learning what could be improved instead of fixating on the error. Positive mental approaches to life in general and baseball specifically. Life was not separate from baseball, everything we did was habit forming good and bad. You are what your consistent mental process and actions say you are. That's the leadership style of Coach Claudio!

I thrived in this environment that really was simple looking back but revolutionary to me at the time-build a relationship with the player; build trust; see what they want; then align it to the team goals and let the person OWN their plan and thus OWN their place at the TEAM table. Accountability, hard work, extra work and communication then all flow in a safe environment. That's what I learned from spending 4 years under Coach Claudio's leadership. That is why our continued friendship has spanned in excess of 25 years. He is the ultimate player's coach; no ego; lead by demonstrating hard work; players have a relationship with him built by the mutual trust he fostered. RESPECT earned in both directions! A BIG reason he is a head coach and has been for 30 plus years (sorry about the inferred age reference coach)!

My hope is that anyone reading this coaches and leads like Coach Claudio. He's a game changer!! The style of leadership and coaching inspires people to be better humans! It's just the way it should be!

******

RAINER NUNEZ
(CARNEGIE MELLON-2018)

It didn't feel like a coach-player relationship. Or at least not like any of the coaches I've ever had in my life. He cared about me beyond the field, and that's something that was invaluable to me.

It was the night before my second to last game of my college career, and I was set to pitch the next morning. Stupid college kid, doing stupid college things…and long story short…I find myself on the floor in agonizing ankle pain. I stand up and limp over to the nearest wall, and the FIRST thing that crossed my mind was, I have to let coach know that I got hurt and might not be able to pitch the next day. My text to him said the following "Hey coach, I fell and hurt my ankle, but I'm going to try and heal it for tomorrow morning". That same night the pain was so bad that I was taken to the ER and told that I completely snapped my fibula and had extensive ligament damage in my ankle. As you can probably guess, I did not pitch the next day, BUT I was there in the dug-out, with my crutches and temporary cast, cheering on the guys that didn't do anything stupid the night before.

The whole time I was just beating myself up because I let coach down. I had one job to focus on and didn't do it. Just his reaction and disappointment in not having me play my last games made me feel sad. I knew he was more upset with the situation than me, of course, but for some reason, the fact that I needed reconstructive surgery on my leg, was nowhere on my mind at the time.

When I woke up from surgery, coach was the person I woke up to. He spent hours with me at the hospital. That's the person he is. Like I said, I don't think he was ever upset with me throughout the ordeal at all, but more saddened with something like this happening to me.

Believe it or not, this is just one small example that outlines the relationship that coach Claudio and I have. Playing baseball was just a great add-on, but it was more about growing up as a person and modeling my character around someone who truly cared about my growth.

Someone like him, you want to make proud.

******

DARRYL TAN (CARNEGIE MELLON-2015)

My name is Darryl Tan. I had the pleasure of being coached by Claudio for my 4 years at Carnegie Mellon. I've also had the pleasure of getting to know him more throughout the years keeping in touch. Claudio is not only a great coach but a great person as well. On the field, he always had the right thing to say; whether it was a motivational talk, or a reassuring hand. Off the field, Claudio not only got to know me well, but also looked actively to help me in any way possible, whether professionally or personally. Through the years, his simple check-in texts during the holidays are always a welcome sight and is an example of how he truly cares for the relationships he has built over the years. He is a compassionate and kind person, which translates wonderfully to his relationships with his current players as well.

******

TYLER SCANLON
(CARNEGIE MELLON-2015)

Coach Claudio can definitely be described as a "player's coach." This is not because he allows his players to get away with things that other coaches might not. Claudio takes the time to develop personal relationships with his players so that he can understand them on a level that goes far beyond the game of baseball. Those relationships that he fosters with his players hold a dual purpose in both his and his players' lives as his impact is seen on and off the field. Getting to know his players allows him to learn what makes them "tick." This in turn gives

him the ability to motivate and instill discipline in ways that are unique for each individual player that he coaches. Bringing out the best in his players on the field is something he takes pride in, but there is nothing more important to Claudio than developing his players into young men. College is a transformative period of life, and he uses the game of baseball to teach life lessons which can apply to being a good friend, husband, and father when his players move on to the next chapter. Claudio remains interested in his players far beyond their time in his program and frequently checks in on them and their families. His players are what mean the most to him, a true player's coach.

******

BRYANT BACKUS
(CARNEGIE MELLON- 2018)

Coach Claudio and I had a strong player coach relationship. I think the reason for this stems from the fact that Claudio cared about his players as people before players. He created personal connections with his players and made the effort to learn about their lives as well as let his players into his own personal life as well. We still keep in touch even after my graduation and find time to catch up. It also showed in his coaching style. He never screamed at his players or punished them for making mistakes but was sure to let you know of them and correct you. His ability to connect with players allowed him to build strong relationships. Coach Claudio always put his all into coaching and wanted the best for his players and the team and as a player you could really appreciate that. For these reasons among others, Claudio was one of my favorite coaches.

******

ZAC ETTENSHON
(CARNEGIE MELLON-2018)

During my four years playing under Claudio he helped me grow tremendously as a baseball player; he helped me be the best version of myself as a player and keep hitting simple. But more importantly, over time we also developed a personal relationship off the field. It was clear he cared deeply about me and my teammates not just as players but as people. I've had many coaches throughout my life, and Claudio is the only one I continue to get dinner with and golf with to this day. I really appreciate the fact that our relationship extends beyond baseball.

******

KEVIN YOST (CARNEGIE MELLON-2021)

To me, Claudio's strongest coaching belief is preaching simplicity. He recognizes that no player is the same, whether that be due to strengths or weaknesses in athleticism, mindset, skillset, or mechanics. He simply reinforces the fundamentals and allows each player's unique mechanics and athleticism to complement the fundamentals, so long as it does not obstruct their growth. This style of coaching is reassuring and helps me play with more confidence, as it demonstrates that Claudio has faith in my ability as a player.

******

NICK HALBEDL (CARNEGIE MELLON-2018)

I played for Claudio from 2015-2018, and it was one of my favorite experiences while in college. What made our relationship as a player and coach great was that I could tell he genuinely cared about my life off the field. When I would arrive for practice, our first conversation usually wasn't about baseball. Instead it would be about how my classes were going, how my family was, or sometimes it was just talking about our favorite local restaurants. It was these conversations that made our on-field relationship even better, because I knew that any suggestions or advice were always in my best interest. Claudio wanted me to succeed because it was the success of me and my teammates that made him happy, not his individual success as a coach. But by forming solid relationships with us, great on-field results for our team came naturally. Even after I graduated from Carnegie Mellon Claudio and I have stayed in touch, which further proves that our relationship was much bigger than baseball.

******

SAMEER KOLLURI
(CARNEGIE MELLON- 2018)

For Coach

My relationship with Coach Claudio started at Carnegie Mellon's first practice my freshman year. Having played baseball all my life, I joined the team to continue playing at a competitive level, while meeting new people. Early on, I noticed Coach's approach to running practice. As far as coaching some random college club baseball team, he never seemed to be disengaged and uninterested. The advice and tips started coming out on the first day.

During high school, I injured my throwing arm to the point of being able to pitch only one inning before it would go numb. Baseball was a major part of my life as I was playing year-round, so not having my arm was a huge blow to my confidence – on and off the field. I still wanted to pitch, so I had a bit of a love-hate relationship with the game. I told Coach that I could only pitch one inning, to which he accepted at face value. Looking back, I believe that changed the first game Coach put me in a game.

It was a save situation against West Virginia and we had a big lead. After being told I was going in, I got nervous and asked to be brought in with an out. Again, Coach accepted what I said and let that happen. I ended up making it a close game, giving up a couple runs in the end. After we had won the game, Coach pulled me aside and gave me the talk I needed to hear for a long time. Having not known him for long, I was hoping he was not too upset. Against my expectations, he calmly explained why I should not have been so nervous. He wanted me to see that, of all the things to be afraid of in life, a baseball game was not worth the worry. He assured me of my ability, but also wanted me to see my own skill for what it was and be confident in myself. After that meeting, I decided I had to make a change for my team, but first and foremost, for me. After that point, I ended up pitching more innings and the team ended up having successful seasons to follow.

During my years at Carnegie Mellon, I was always looking forward to practice and games and meeting Coach. I was able to improve my game, while looking forward to our various discussions, which ranged from how our day went to the economy and current events. He was never a hard-ass and he never wasted our time. He was able to strike the balance between a mentor and a sincere and genuine friend. As I said earlier, I had initially expected him to not care much about some club baseball team, but he never held anything back. He would always show that he appreciated your time and effort in practice and games and it was evidenced by his high energy (walking miles while coaching third base) and constant coaching (giving advice in between swings at the plate). Fighting against the rain of Pittsburgh, he spent hours preparing our fields for either practice or games. In our successes, he was cheerfully teary-eyed and, in our losses, he was steadfast. He was someone the players could rally behind in victory and defeat. Because of how much he genuinely cared for us, I was, and still am, able to trust and respect him.

Since my graduation 2 years ago, my relationship with Coach is still going strong. My ex-teammates and I will go to games and grab dinner with him when we can. While life get busier, we still manage to stay in touch. While we can still talk baseball, I am happy our relationship was able to transcend the game.

******

CAM DIVELY (CARNEGIE MELLON-2018)

I have had many coaches with many different styles. All of them have helped shape me as a ballplayer. However, aside from my father (who shall always be the most revered Coach in my life), there is only one other coach whose advice I can recall with complete clarity. That is Coach Claudio.

The best example of this (though there are many) occurred during my first year on the team. I was a bright-eyed freshman desperate to make an impact, and this translated into an equally strong desire to avoid screwing up. We were getting ready to play one our rivals, and Coach was starting me at catcher. This would be my first time behind the dish while playing at CMU, and my pitcher was an upperclassman who had been dominant in the league for several years. I was extremely nervous - both at the prospect of poor pitch-calling or our ace and the possibility that I would fail to block wild pitches or overthrow second on a steal attempt. In essence, I was focused on all the ways I could fail.

I must not have been good at concealing my worries, since after the first inning Coach pulled me aside. He looked me straight in the eye and said "Don't be afraid to take charge back there. You're the catcher - you can see everything happening on the field, and everyone depends on your calls. I wouldn't have put you there unless I had complete confidence in you, so don't doubt yourself." That simple vote of confidence from Coach was exactly what I needed. My concerns vanished and once again I was focused solely on the task at hand - helping the team win.

I went on to play for four years at CMU, facing every type of challenging opponent or difficult situation. But I never doubted myself or my abilities again. Coach addressed that problem in my very first game, and I carried that confidence throughout my career at CMU.

Thanks Coach, for having confidence in me when I did not. Your advice may only have taken a few seconds to deliver but I haven't forgotten it, and I don't think I ever will.

******
DAN EVANS (CARNEGIE MELLON-2016)

Looking back on my baseball career, I can safely say that every major life lesson to learn, can be learned in a dugout. That was especially true for my time playing for Coach Claudio, who taught me much more about life than he did about baseball.

Coming to CMU, I had been raised in an elitist, socially crisp environment my whole life, both as a student and as a baseball player. Claudio's upbringing and background were much different from mine, which made it all the more insightful to learn from his experience as a coach, entrepreneur, family man, and all-around professional. His approach to coaching was also much different from what I had known. He demonstrated trust and commitment in a grounded, familial way that no coach (or instructor of any kind) had shown to me before. Some of my fondest memories of college were my times in the batting cage, where Claudio and I would shoot the breeze while I took my cuts - only to be interrupted by him correcting something small about my technique. And some of my hardest memories were when I didn't perform well on the field. In my whirlwind of starting college, making new friends, adjusting to life away from home, and trying to earn my place on the team, his support was an anchor that gave me something to look forward to each practice, and to be reminded of when things seemed a little overwhelming.

Most of all, I credit Claudio with showing me that true satisfaction in life comes from being trusted with responsibility - both on and off the field. My baseball career in high school was rocky and disappointing, mainly because of the stick-up-the-behind attitude that all of my coaches had. After batting .609 my freshman year, I dislocated my shoulder the night before opening night of my sophomore junior varsity season, so I missed most of that season. Because of unwritten rules, I was then cut from my varsity team in the most infuriating way. My coaches waxed poetic about my work ethic and talent but gave the spot to a returning senior who didn't show up for any "optional" off season practices because he had been on the team the year before. I never got the chance to prove them wrong, as I dislocated my shoulder again the following year and had to miss the whole season. Because of this rocky road, I had come to accept a particular "mold" of the attitude of a baseball coach - uncompromising, non-supporting (unless you were getting scouted), self-righteous, and caught up in self-destructive traditions. But since they coached the sport I loved, I would have to endure them.

Claudio didn't just break that mold - he blasted it into another dimension.

Fast forward to when I walked on to the CMU baseball team. Given my playing history in high school, I was hoping for a few at-bats as a backup, and maybe earning a slot in the starting lineup by junior year. But less than a week after the first practice of my freshman year, Claudio told me I was going to bat cleanup and start in the outfield. He told me that he trusted me to get the job done, and that he would support me as I faced this new challenge. Looking back years later, I now realize that that was my first taste of genuine, adult self-responsibility. Claudio's trust motivated me to perform to the very best of my ability, to earn a higher place by proving myself. And his continued support of my professional development, both on and off the field, was a key factor in my success as an athlete, an academic, a musician, and a member of my campus community. Even when I had to pull back from playing baseball because of other commitments, Claudio continued to trust my judgment and encourage my career development.

If you get the privilege to work with the right people, baseball ends up being so much more than just baseball. While my career on Claudio's team was far too short, it made an enormous impact on how I view the world, how I interact with people who are different from me, and how I face new challenges both personally and professionally. I am grateful for his continued friendship and encourage anyone who can to learn from his example.

******

MIKE TERRICK (CARNEGIE MELLON- 2014)

"I've been asked to talk about my relationship with Claudio, and honestly it's been very hard to choose the right words. What do you say about the man that made you who you are today? I'm not just talking on the field, he helped me learn what life was about before I had even considered it. A short biography on me, I grew up the lanky but somewhat not athletic kid. I was never good enough to start in high school, but never bad enough to not be a bench player. When I came to

CMU, I had no idea that there was even a baseball team until I saw that one of my classmates had a glove during our lecture. I turned around and jokingly asked where his game was after the lecture. That was when he informed me that CMU had a team and that practice was after our lecture. After that, I ran back to my dorm room to grab my glove. I had never been so nervous, but everyone welcomed me with open arms. Through the months and years, we trained a few days a week in a facility that had the same space as two rows of an office cubicle. But we made the absolute best of it. Claudio was always working with the team in the batting cage, and despite what a lot of coaches do these days he never tried to conform someone's swing to some random MLB player's swing. No, he was always someone that knew that he had to help people play the hand that they were dealt and was able to customize everyone's swing to what he knew was the best for them. He took my swing, which in high school was called a "Frankenstein swing" to a swing that could actually compete at a college level. This is a very long account, but that's just what you get when talking about the coach of your team, as well as the coach of your life, and I'm just disappointed that I didn't have space to say more.

****

JIMMY STEDMAN
(CARNEGIE MELLON- 2010)

I never had a coach with the amount of passion and emotion that Claudio would bring to every practice and every game. It was inspiring to see someone so invested in his team and in the success of each of his players.

Aside from knowing baseball inside and out, his commitment to his players on and off the field is what made Claudio a great leader. His investment and genuine interest in each of us didn't stop at just a player-coach relationship, nor did it stop after graduation. We still catch up around holidays, even if it is a simple text to check in.

I have great respect for Claudio. He set the tone for the team. Being at such an academically demanding school, it could be easy to get overwhelmed with schoolwork and put everything else on the back burner. Our guys did not do that, and I attribute that to Claudio's example. He came to every practice and game, 100% focused.

I spent hours at a hospital with Claudio, late into the night, after our team president dislocated his shoulder in a game. His level of concern was as though it was his own kid that was hurt.

After suffering my own shoulder injury that sidelined me for about a season and a half, I still went to every practice and game possible to run the pitching machine, catch in while someone hit flies and grounders, keep score or coach first base because I wanted to stay a part of his team. Thanks to Claudio and the great group of guys we had, being on that team created some of the best memories I have of my college years. Thanks to Claudio and the great group of guys we had, being on that team created some of the best memories I have of my college years.

****

James Langhauser—Carnegie Mellon University—Class of 2010

I played for Claudio for 4 years from 2006-2010 and have stayed very close friends since. When I think back at my time playing for Claudio there are dozens of stories and lessons that stand out in my memories. Stories that come to mind include protecting his starters when we needed to drag a deer off the field, the steal "signal" that morphed into a shrug and warning the new assistant coach not to come talk to me when I was pissed on the mound. But above all two things stand out, first is his no bullshit approach to coaching and second is relentlessly following your passion and doing what you love.

It was my first day of practice my freshman year at Carnegie Mellon, after warmups we went right into BP. I was the first up to bat and embarrassingly swung and missed at the first pitch, and ended up with an overall mediocre round of BP. After I bat, I head out to center field and shag down fly balls. Then I see Claudio jogging out to me, in what will come to be known to me as the "Claudio jog". He calls me over and says, "James, you're going to leadoff and play centerfield for us." I didn't know it at the time, but this was perfectly emblematic of Claudio's no bullshit approach. To be clear, this is not the "no fun allowed" approach many coaches embrace, but more accurately just cutting things that don't add value. He could have started me further down the lineup and made me earn my spot at the top of the order, but why? Throughout my time at CMU, this was demonstrated over an over again, whether it was how he ran infield / outfield warmups, not religiously tracking pitch counts, or hanging out with players off the field. Claudio did nothing just for show and refused to conform to the traditional status quo of coaching but rather focused on getting the best out of those on the field. This is a methodology that I carry with me into my career today, I always try to cut out the activities that are for show and focus on the aspects of my job that create the most value.

The second aspect is clear within minutes of knowing Claudio, he follows his passion and will stop at nothing to do what he loves. At any point in time Claudio has at least a half dozen jobs from coaching, to scout, to radio host to landscaping. He doesn't do all these jobs because he has to but because he is passionate about them. He always had the dream of being in professional baseball and relentlessly pursued that dream every day. His passion and motivation are obvious in the way he approaches the job as coach at CMU and is contagious, but most importantly, it makes you want to find something you are equally passionate about and go all-in. This is a valuable lesson that is especially important for college students who are trying everyday to figure out what they are doing with the rest of their lives. Not only do I try to live this lesson in my daily life, but also look forward to teaching my kids this same lesson and imploring them to go all in on their dreams.

Overall, I look back at my time at CMU playing for Claudio fondly and try to live these lessons in my life each day. This time helped shape me as a person and lead me on the right path, but more importantly I still consider Claudio a close friend and mentor.

****
John Schuman—
Carnegie Mellon University ---2020

The most inspiring, heartfelt coach you could ask for: Claudio Reilsono, my coach of four years at Carnegie Mellon University, taught me more than just how to be a better ball player. He continues to show me what it means to care about that which I'm passionate about. He constantly reminds me to be gracious, giving and never stop working to be who I want to be, because eventually work will no longer feel like work.That mentality stuck with me throughout school, as I pursued what made me happy rather than what others expected of me. It extended on the ball field, as every practice and game was both a mission and an opportunity to pursue a craft.

Claudio Reilsono knows baseball better than almost anyone. He knows the scouting, the coaching and his players. He won't force you out of what you're comfortable with as long as you give yourself an opportunity to be successful in the way you operate. Instead of attempting to rewire his players, he approaches coaching from a perspective of tweaking that which needs fixing. An example would be his comparison of twin baseball players with different batting stances. As long as they're throwing their hands at the pitcher, staying closed and finishing long there is potential for that swing.

For me, Claudio had a small checklist of things that I should keep in mind at the plate. They involved embracing my power through a small elbow adjustment as to be more square to the baseball, as well as stepping through my throws and swings for both better accuracy and power.Claudio will also let you know when you're doing something right, and is often encouraging of his players even beyond their playing ability. That's because he cares about his team, his players, and most importantly the people who show up and show passion for the game.

In many ways, Claudio was there for me throughout my entire college career, starting from before I even joined the team. He was welcoming when I showed an interest to play, even granting me a meeting with the captain of the team during one of the team's Spring doubleheaders. He expressed my importance to the team in a surprising way when I skipped a double header my freshman year; as a result I was benched in the following series, and had the support of my team and my coach in understanding what we could accomplish together rather than apart. This was a turning point in my time playing CMU baseball, as it showed me the passion that it would take to be successful not only in baseball, but in school and life as well. As the old adage goes, eighty percent of success is showing up.

As I got older, Claudio became even more of a mentor and friend to me, inviting me for off-hand lunches to talk about life, family and baseball. He also invited me to be on his talk show many times, and I was able to participate in and talk baseball on a podcast, something I never anticipated. Claudio opens his heart to the Pittsburgh community in many ways, and is an inspiration for how any person should lead a passionate life centered on family, friends and appreciating one's craft.I'm grateful to have Claudio Reilsono as my coach, a dear friend and a mentor. His influence on my life goes beyond the diamond. My perception of family, the college experience, and my outlook on the future have all been influenced by the many ways Claudio helped shape who I am as a person today. For that I'll be eternally grateful, and hope to call Claudio a life-long friend.

****

Morgan Dively --
Carnegie Mellon University (2019)

My time playing for Coach, among other important things, primarily taught me the value of leadership through hard work. Leaders can have many qualities which land them in their role – charisma, intelligence, experience, raw talent or ability – but most are not earned. They are the blessings you are born with or they're what you've garnered in times preceding your role as a leader. The only thing which can justify and solidify an individual as a leader is their work ethic, and this is something I certainly learned from Coach. Rain or shine (or on occasion in Pittsburgh, snow), Coach was at practice before anyone and was usually the last to leave. If there was a hard rain on Friday before a Saturday doubleheader, you could bet Coach was at the field with a rake and a pick-up truck full of diamond-dry as the sun rose. He worked hard to stay invested in his players' success off the field as well – checking in with text messages, meetings in the off-season, and more. Those kinds of qualities in a coach are the kind that make a team want to play harder and improve. When I had the privilege of being one of two team captains my senior year, they were the qualities I tried to model my own actions after. I tried always to be the first to arrive at practice and the last to leave. I made sure that all the freshmen hoping to get a chance to pitch a bullpen at the end of practice could always find an enthusiastic catcher in me. If someone needed some batting practice, I was happy to throw to them. They're little things, but showing humility and working hard when in a position of leadership establishes a culture that can't be beat. And after you graduate, they are the qualities that will set you apart and help you succeed in the real world. It is why I'm grateful for my friendship with Coach and the example he sets for all his players.

I'd be remiss if I didn't also include my favorite sayings of his –

"The best feeling in the world is lying exhausted on the field of victory. The second-best feeling in the world is lying exhausted on the field after defeat."

"How do you eat an elephant? One bite at a time."

"Play the hand your dealt."

Paraphrasing the best hitting advice you can give someone: "Don't worry about how technically good your swing is – see the ball early, see it the whole way through, and trust your hands."

****

My Coach and Friend Claudio Reilsono:

When I think of one of the most influential people in my life, I consider Claudio Reilsono as one of those distinctive individuals. I was blessed to have Claudio as an extraordinary high school baseball coach during some of the most formative years of my life. Not only was Claudio a fantastic coach and leader, he was an impeccable motivator, energizer, compassionate, and loving person that demanded perfection not through the iron fist mentality, but kind-heartedness. His mastery of understanding of how to connect with young men to always get the best out of them was exceptional. Most importantly, he connected with his players because of his genuine love for them. Claudio's leadership was not always tied to baseball and or coaching exclusively, but a friend and lending hand and ear in times of need. You see, one of the most special gifts that Claudio possessed was the investment in the minds and hearts of young men to be successful. Not necessarily only tied to a nine-inning competition on the diamond. Certainly, through the game of baseball, many a lesson were learned. However, more importantly they were transitional to the game of life. I once had heard of the importance to always have a mentor in one's life, somebody that can be called upon for advice to have traveled the path of life beforehand. I can say undeniable, Claudio has been one of those mentors in my lifetime.

****

Michael Ruperto

Quaker Valley – Class of 89'

I joined the Carnegie Mellon Baseball Club on a cold spring afternoon. The team was taking batting practice in a small indoor section of the upper campus gym. I introduced myself as a catcher and immediately caught the attention of Claudio. He came over and introduced himself with a glove in his hand and asked to warm up with me. I knew I was essentially trying out for the team at that point. I had a good arm as was sure to show it. Claudio couldn't help but grin after my first throw, and I knew I had passed the first inspection. I'll never forget that first day on the team as it really embodies the type of coach Claudio was. He was involved, collaborative, and expressive.

Claudio loves to be involved in every aspect of the game. The same drive to warm up with me first hand on my first day drives him to pitch batting practice, demonstrate techniques, hit ground balls and pop flys (even if he still needs work on hitting flies to the catcher). During practice he has dozens of different conversations and interactions between each player. He cares for you as a whole person and not just as a player. He asks about how your family is doing and is willing to listen to whatever may be bothering you. My time at Carnegie Mellon was difficult for me with lots of struggle and self-doubt. Claudio was always willing to meet up and chat, usually grabbing some pancakes at Pamela's Diner. Claudio was one of the few people that believed in me, even when I didn't, and was critical in getting me through those years.

While Claudio was very hands-on, he was also very collaborative. He trusted the input of his players and would let me call entire games on my own. He also had a reason for why he would do everything and was always willing to explain. He truly valued your buy-in to concept and was always willing to work with his players. This also tied into his also experimental nature. Claudio is not one to force a player into a mold but will find solutions that work for them. He might have you try a couple of methods, which can be further fine-tuned based on your feedback or altered entirely if they just aren't working. Growth as a player under Claudio's tutelage was very natural and organic.

Claudio's grin gave away his evaluation of me the first time we met, and in general it was

usually extremely easy to tell how he was feeling. He will be among the first to jump and cheer for his players that hit a home run or laugh at the jokes being told in the dugout. While disappointment and loss are also an equal part in sports, Claudio is quick to reflect the somberness of the setting while managing to frame them in a constructive way. The Carnegie Mellon Baseball Club was a team that had to lose a lot before it started to win. Claudio's ability to be disappointed by a loss, but not let it get him or the rest of the team down is a contributing factor to what eventually turned things around.

It was privilege to have a coach like Claudio while attending Carnegie Mellon, and I am honored to call him a friend to this day. The qualities that make Claudio a great coach are all derived from the elements that make him a great person.

****

Brian Tabata—Carnegie Mellon University--2010

I met Claudio back in 1989 when he was assistant coach at Penn State Beaver. I remember he and I talking in a parking lot after I had a tough game. He took the time to help me with hitting. He was talking a mile a minute and as passionate as he could possibly talk. Then he had this thick notebook full of notes he shared with me. He always believed in me. We still talk to this day. About baseball, business and about life. I am so glad we can call each other friend.

****

Tom Grossetti—1989 Penn State Beaver

"I was fortunate to play college baseball with Claudio as a coach. He was more than just a coach. He was a mentor and a friend who saw his players as more than athletes to take the field on game day. He was genuinely interested in forming a personal relationship with us and was ready to provide advice on whatever subject or questions we had. Claudio understood that we were there because we loved the game of baseball and not because we were making a career out of it.

I know what it feels like to have a coach who makes you hate the game, and I'm happy to say Claudio did the complete opposite. I looked forward to every practice and game because I knew the environment he fostered was one of camaraderie and brotherhood and not one with an aggressive or dog-eat-dog mentality, and I know it worked. This environment created a team that wanted to play and play hard because we wanted to, not because we were forced to.

I want to thank Claudio for having me enjoy my last few years of competitive baseball and for forming a lifelong friendship. Regardless of how much or how little we talk, I know Claudio will always be someone who will be there to lend some advice, tell a story, or just be available to chat."

****

Alex Walenczyk—2017
-Carnegie Mellon University

After reading all of the notes my players sent me for the book, I cannot tell you how deeply moved I was. I am surprised, yet glad that they remember the stories, the actions, moments lessons and the quotes. I remember my Dad Olindo always telling me, " You will attract more bees with honey than you will with mustard. So be good to people." He was right, and these kind words prove it. As I have said, I want them to enjoy playing for our team, and for me. When they graduate, I want them to hate the fact they are leaving the team, and me. The words they penned is more of a reflection on the type of people that I have had and continue to have to coach. They wrote these words from "The Heart up, not the Neck up". I cannot thank them enough.

The Guys present me with a Birthday Cake/Cookie. What a special group of people. (Photo courtesy of the author)

****
Ryan Comes--Carnegie Mellon University 2008

"Out of all the coaches that I had playing baseball for almost 20 years, Coach Claudio was the one who went that extra mile and showed how much he cared about his players. Claudio knows the game and how to make players better than anyone I ever played for, but it's how he goes about coaching that sets him apart. We spent three years at Carnegie Mellon working together to build a winning team. More than that though, Claudio came in and took over a program that never had any stability and turned it into a team with a real bond amongst the players and coach. I knew that I could call him about anything and he was going to have my back. Knowing that you have that kind of support makes fighting through morning practices, frigid March games, and the uphill battle that is winning at a school without baseball facilities of its own worthwhile. It took some time, but we were a much better team and a much better program when I graduated than when Claudio took over. I was so proud to see them make the playoffs two straight years as a reward for the decade of hard work Claudio and his players have put into the program. Claudio IS the Carnegie Mellon baseball program and hundreds of kids for the past 15 years have improved as ballplayers and been better prepared for life after college from having the opportunity to play for him."

ACKNOWLEDGEMENTS

Some especially important people I would like to thank:

- David Finoli
- Lizzie Schinkel
- David Angeron
- Jodi Valasquez
- Lynda Reilsono
- Ida Reilsono

John Melvin Publishing. Thank you for all of your help and your belief in this book. I am honored to be a part of the JMP family.

John Calipari for being such a great role model and for your kindness toward me and my family.

Jim Valvano for the IMPACT in every aspect of my life.

Ryan Comes. Thank you to my players who wrote such kind testimonials:

- Wade Brogdon
- Dom Perry
- Rainer Nunez
- Collin Sample
- Tyler Scanlon
- Cam Dively
- Sameer Kolluri
- Nick Halbedl

- Zac Ettenshon
- Tim Liu
- Kevin Yosy
- Daryl Tan
- Mike Terrick
- Bryant Backus
- Dan Evans
- Jon Coens
- James Langhauser
- John Schuman
- Mike Ruperto
- Brian Tabata
- Morgan Dively
- Tom Grossetti
- Alex Walenczyk

I would like to thank all of the schools, coaches and companies who hired me. I appreciate the opportunities you gave me.

I must thank ALL of my players. Thank you for the time you put in, the passion you gave and the kindness, respect, and feelings you showed me.

James L. Gamble. Thank you for allowing my dreams to come true. You truly are Santa Claus

Thank you to the BEST wife anyone could ever have. You really did have me at hello. Thank you and Love you Lynda.

If the Good Lord would have asked me to write down the exact daughter, I would have wanted I could not have come up with a better daughter than you. Ida, love you and so proud of you.

Mom (Ida), Dad (Olindo). "If you ever see a turtle on top of a fence post you know he didn't get there alone" I would not have the life or career I am having without you both. Thank you is not enough. Love you is not enough. Everyone will know more about you in my next book!

My prayers pretty much consist of just saying "Thank you" I have a great group of friends who are always supportive of me. Vince Kaplack, Nick Kaplack, Rick Mitchell, Eric Jackson Lurie, Brian Kaplan, Bobby Farrington, Luther Dupree Jr., " Smokin" Jim Frazier, Vinny Paz and Donny Lalonde. My cousin Chris who was always supportive of no matter what I wanted to do, thank you. As I said, I am Blessed to have had and have great friends, great parents, have a great wife, great daughter, I am even had a great dog...Grover! Thank you to all the Coaches, Leaders I have studied and learned from. Again, I have been truly Blessed.

ABOUT CLAUDIO

Claudio Reilsono is the Head Baseball Coach at Carnegie Mellon University as well as the GM/Professional baseball Scout for the Global Scouting Bureau. Claudio started his career in 1983 at the age of 18 as the Assistant Baseball Coach at his Alma Matter Quaker Valley. In 1988 Reilsono was named Head Coach at QV. He moved on to be the Assistant Coach at Penn State Beaver in 1989. In 1990 he was named Head Coach at Penn State Beaver and his team won a Collegiate Championship. Claudio was also assistant at Community College of Beaver County, Quigley Catholic High School and Duquesne University as well as the Head Coach at Community College of Beaver County.

In 2005 Claudio was named Head Coach at Carnegie Mellon University and under his tenure the team has had its most successful seasons including 2 consecutive Conference Championships in 2015 & 2016. Reilsono is the All Time Leader in Baseball Wins at CMU.

As a Professional Scout, Claudio has assisted in professional player signings all over the world and was named General Manager of the Global Scouting Bureau in 2002.

Claudio is also a Professional Hitting Instructor, conducts his own Hitting camps in several States, produced a Hitting video in 2003, is a hired instructor at many baseball camps and is the Lead Instructor for the CRONS Brand baseball Camps.

Claudio is the Co-Host of "Steel City Sports" TV show and the Host of " Ring Talk" Pittsburgh's only TV Boxing Show. He is also the Host of "The Claudio Reilsono Show" (Podcast Show)-(claudioreilsono.com). He also serves as a color commentator in both baseball & boxing events. Served as a radio analyst for a Major League Baseball Post Season Show on WMBA Radio.

Reilsono has also been a writer for Boxing publications such as RealBoxing.com (RI/ Mass.) Sports Review Magazine (RI/Mass.) Kids Sports Magazine (Pittsburgh) & Pittsburgh Sports Report. From 2010-11 he was a co-owner of the MMA Promotion Company Paramount Fighting.

Claudio also started his own company, "Claudio Reilsono Enterprises" which has under its umbrella, Baseball training, Motivational Speaking, Film, Books, Podcast and TV projects, Celebrity Placement co. and a Landscaping business.

In 2011 Claudio was voted into the Carnegie Mellon University Baseball Hall of Fame and was awarded the "Willie Stargell MVP Lifetime Achievement Award". 2014 was voted in to the "Steel City Sports" Hall of Fame and in 2016 was named "Italian Coach of the Year" By the National Italian American Sports Hall of Fame (Pittsburgh Chapter). Inducted into the "Pittsburgh Sportsline Hall of Fame" in 2020.

Claudio is also invited to participate in many Celebrity Golf outings and other events.

A Documentary is in development about Claudio's life & career. His story has been included in 3 books including a book written by Former Philadelphia Eagle & Subject of the Movie "Invincible" Vince Papale "Be Invincible"

Claudio's parents were both born in Calabria Italy... Father Olindo, Falerna, and Mother Ida, Nocera

He is married to Lynda (22 years) and they have one daughter Ida (19) Who is Attending the University of Pittsburgh and is a Member of the Pitt Color Guard... They reside in Sewickley, PA.

Claudio is available for:

- ⛰ Speaking Engagements
- ⛰ Coaching/Consulting
- ⛰ Media Interviews
- ⛰ Corporate Outings

To Contact Claudio:

reilsono16@msn.com

claudioreilsono.com

Twitter: @claudioreilsono

With Ida & Lynda..Together for ever

www.ingramcontent.com/pod-product-compliance
Lightning Source LLC
Chambersburg PA
CBHW071451080526
44587CB00014B/2062